Myth, Magic, and Farce

Four Multicultural Plays

by Sterling Houston

Edited and with an Introduction by Sandra M. Mayo

University of North Texas Press
Denton, Texas

High Yello Rose ©1992 by Sterling Houston
Isis in Nubia ©1993 by Sterling Houston
Black Lily and White Lily ©1997 by Sterling Houston
Miranda Rites ©1994 by Sterling Houston
Introduction © 2005 by Sandra M. Mayo
Printed in the United States of America.

10 9 8 7 6 5 4 3 2 1

The paper used in this book meets the minimum requirements of the American National Standard for Permanence of Paper for Printed Library Materials, z39.48.1984. Binding materials have been chosen for durability.

Library of Congress Cataloging-in-Publication Data

Houston, Sterling, 1945–
    Myth, magic, and farce : four multicultural plays / by Sterling Houston ; edited and with an introduction by Sandra M. Mayo.
        p. cm.
    ISBN 1-57441-187-X (pbk. : alk. paper)
    1. Multiculturalism--Drama. 2. Pluralism (Social sciences)--Drama. 3. Cultural relations--Drama. 4. Ethnic relations--Drama. 5. Race relations--Drama. I. Mayo, Sandra Marie, 1947- II. Title.
    PS3608.O875M98 2005
    812'.6--dc22
                                                2004019925

Photo on cover of Cassandra Small and Kevin Evans in *Isis in Nubia* is by Gary M. Perkins.

Other plays by Sterling Houston:

Harlem: A Renaissance Remembered, 1986
The Modernization of Sainthood, 1988
A Brief History of American Song, 1988
The Late Late Show at the Gilded Cage, 1989
A'Ielia, 1990
Kool Jams, 1990
Cheap Talk, 1992
Driving Wheel, 1992
Womandingo, 1992
La Frontera, 1993
Santo Negro, 1995
The Alien Show, Kool Jams '99, 1997
Miss Bowden's Dream, 1998
LeGriffon, 2000
Cameoland, 2002

Contents

Sterling Houston
Photo by Rueben Njaa

Introduction

Sterling Houston is a prolific, innovative African American playwright. He is a native of San Antonio who has lived and worked in the Alamo City since returning to his home in 1981. During a career spanning several decades in professional theatre as actor, technician, and writer in San Antonio, New York, and San Francisco he has worked with some of the greatest practitioners of modern theatre, including Charles Ludlam, Sam Shepard, and George C. Wolfe. His plays are known for their biting social commentary, burlesque humor, and intensive musical ideas. Houston is the artistic director and writer-in-residence for Jump-Start Performance Company, a not-for-profit, presenting-and-producing theatre collective, dedicated to the exploration of alternative viewpoints.

Houston is a man of his time, of his region—a South Texas playwright. His plays, over twenty produced, speak of the Southwestern experience, the Black, Hispanic (Mexican), and European American experience. His work is an answer to the call for a contemporary theatre that mirrors the diversity of our culture. The plays are the voice of the male (sensitive and macho), the strong, weak, and independent female, the homosexual and the straight.

Sterling Houston is a unique talent in San Antonio and the South. He joined Jump-Start Performance Company in 1988 as a performer. In 1989 he became its writer-in-residence, in 1990 its administrative director, and shortly thereafter its artistic director, a position he still holds in 2003. For over fourteen years he has had a productive relationship with the founder of the company and director of many of the productions, and longtime executive director, Steve Bailey.

Steve Bailey recognized and encouraged his writing talent when he brought Houston in to perform with the Jump-Start Performance Company on a work called, *It's About Going.* The improvisational nature of the work highlighted Houston's writing potential. When Bailey began making Jump-Start more versatile, and more multicultural, Houston moved from guest artist to regular company member. Over the years, his work has become "iconographic of Jump-Start,"[1] the primary producer of over 20 of his plays: including *Womandingo, Kool Jams, High Yello Rose, Isis in Nubia, Driving Wheel, Miranda Rites, La Frontera,* and *Cameoland.*

Jump-Start Performance Company's audiences are as versatile as the artists at work in the company. They are a company of approximately 20 core artists who vary in ethnicity, aesthetic approach, and artistic disciplines: visual artists, videographers, actors, dancers, designers, writers, and musicians. They each have a special focus that attracts a group of loyal followers. Their production of *La Nueves Tamaleras* by Alicia Mena, which appeals to the Mexican American community, sells out annually. *Big, Bad, and Beautiful,* by Alicia Fernandez, is a work written by, for, and about women of size. Some audience members think Jump-Start is a gay company because they have seen work that focuses on gay issues and gay history. Others think it is an African American company because they have seen works focusing on African American issues. The company annually produces two to four "major" company works and a number of full-length works-in-progress. They are committed to the creation of art that is a lasting voice of many diverse cultures and have consciously fostered a multicultural image reflective of San Antonio's multicultural community.

Sterling Houston's body of work exemplifies Jump-Start's spirit of inclusiveness. *Santo Negro* is one of the examples of his interest in crossing borders. The subject of the drama, Saint Martin de Porres, is a Latino icon, but he was also African. His father was a conquistador and his mother a West African Yoruba. Houston lets the audience see the juxtaposition and mixing of cultures.

Houston's cultural identity is broad. He is connected to his region as well as to his race. He knows he is a black man in a white-dominated society, but his experiences in multicultural San Antonio and on the east and west coasts forged a broader view of himself as a person in the world. His nontraditional lifestyle has allied him with those he identifies as misfits, from the Ridiculous Theatre companies in New York, where members were black, Puerto Rican, white, gay, and straight, to San Francisco and San Antonio with Jump-Start. He said of his artist companions in New York, "We were all avant-gardist, outsiders, and misfits in the wider community."[2]

Houston writes primarily to explore things for himself. He tries to include all that he is, and this, in many plays, leads to the autobiographical—as in *Driving Wheel* based on his relationship with his father and *Black Lily and White Lily* based on some experiences of his mother. *Cameoland* is a historical blues memory play about African Americans on the East Side of San Antonio before integration, a community in which the playwright thrived as a youth. Many of his plays are set in Texas, San Antonio in particular, because Houston says that is what he knows. He works with ideas that excite him because the commitment is sometimes one or two years. *Cameoland* took three years.

In San Antonio and across the country, Sterling Houston's admirers have been a mixture of the voiceless and the powerful. State Senator Ruth Jones McClendon of San Antonio issued a proclamation in recognition of his contributions to the arts in Texas. Maya Angelou responded to his theatrical interpretation of her poem, *On the Pulse of Morning,* with joyful tears and applause. Sterling reveals that even those he expected to object to his irreverent and sometimes outrageous interpretations, as in *High Yello Rose*, have applauded his fresh look, his attempt to expose lies and distortions.

Over the last 14 years, working from his base at Jump-Start, Houston received a number of local, regional, and national awards and grants that demonstrate the appreciative response of the San Antonio community and a wider community of supporters. He is the favorite artistic son in the Alamo City. In 1990, he received a grant from the City of San Antonio Department of Arts and Cultural Affairs for *Kool Jams,* and the Business Committee for the Arts named him "Artist of the Year" in 1992. In addition, in 1992, he was the winner of the FEAT (Festival of Emerging American Theatre) award for *Womandingo.* He also has received numerous grants from the Texas Commission on the Arts, the National Endowment for the Arts, and the Andy Warhol Foundation, and has won the Alamo Theatre Arts Council Awards for best new play, and the Arts and Letters Award from the San Antonio Public Library, to name a few. Commissions include the Mid-America Arts Alliance of *La Frontera* in 1992 and the St. Philip's College Department of Theatre and Fine Arts of *Miss Bowden's Dream* in 1998. With many honors in between, his most recent (2003) was the funding of *Cameoland* by the Rockefeller Foundation. Houston finds living and working in San Antonio fertile ground for his artistic musings about gender, race, and class: the possessed and the dispossessed.

When the San Antonio Museum of Art commissioned Houston in 1989 to write a theatrical work to highlight the highly acclaimed traveling exhibit, "Hidden Heritage," he was surprised because it was his first formal invitation to write a theatre piece, though theatre had been a major part of his life since the age of 15 in Highlands High School theatre productions. Nevertheless, Houston was ready to write because of his experience not only as a performer but also as a technician who had been a keen observer of great writers on two coasts. Theatre was, thus, a natural written form of expression for him. He had a sense of how to develop character and plot, but also had already developed theatrical preferences, a theatre aesthetic.

New York and San Francisco had proven to be fertile ground for developing Houston's aesthetic. In 1964 the playwright dropped out of college and moved to New York to study acting. He lived on the Lower East Side and fell in with a cadre of radical artists living there and began working as an actor off-Broadway. In 1966, he played a snake (the reptile, not the treacherous person) in the second production of a new company called the Playhouse of the Ridiculous. When Charles Ludlam split with the original Theatre of the Ridiculous Company to form his own group with a similar name, Houston performed with both companies. In New York he appeared in two off-Broadway productions and 12 off-off-Broadway productions, in works by Charles Ludlam, Ronald Tavel, and Tony Preston, directed by John Vaccaro and Harvey Tavel. His record of performances includes more than 20 regional productions in San Francisco, Los Angeles, Chicago, Indianapolis, Philadelphia, and San Antonio.

The New York influence—especially the work of Tavel, Ludlam and Vaccaro—became the foundation for the Houston aesthetic. This aesthetic includes freewheeling sexuality, lushness of presentation, burlesque, cross-dressing, and Brechtian presentational style along with an elaborate use of language, including punsterisms and malapropisms. He enjoys taking a cliché and turning it back around; one of his favorites is "womandingo," the title of one of his wildest farces, a play on "mandingo." Like Charles Ludlam, Houston likes to recycle cultural icons and stereotypes, as in *Miranda Rites* when he resurrects Marilyn Monroe, Carmen Miranda, and Dorothy Dandridge. As Houston states, "All of this has been part of the arsenal."[3]

Houston fell under the spell of the Magic Theatre in San Francisco and the San Francisco Mime Troupe while working as an actor and technician on the west coast. To use his words, he had "great serendipitous relationships with actors and writers,"[4] including those later to become famous like Sam Shepard and David Mamet. His current mission at Jump-Start closely mirrors the mission of the San Francisco Mime Troupe, which says its goal is "combating racial fragmentation by doing work that crosses racial and national borders, that by its very existence sustains a vision of multi-cultural, multi-national community: plays that not only have multi-racial plots, but embody many points of view."[5] A salient example in Houston's work is *La Frontera*, a musical comedy/drama about a Latino family moving into San Antonio's East Side, a historic black neighborhood. However, Houston's work does not have the immediacy sought by the Mime Troupe, a group that develops theatrically topical issues in a grass-roots way, actually going to communities and dramatizing the issues.

Houston's work is similar to that of the San Francisco Mime Troupe and El Teatro Campesino in its quest to give voice to the voiceless. Luis Valdez founded El Teatro Campesino in 1965 as a vehicle to help the striking farm workers in California. His group specialized in *actos* (short comic agitprop pieces), but soon added *corridos* (ballad dramas), and *mitos* (dramatizations of myths) to their repertoire. As in the work of Luis Valdez and his company, Houston rewrites or elaborates on history and myth. Houston's plays are explorations of myth, of mythology: *Isis in Nubia*, traditional ancient myth, or the myth of history, as in *High Yello Rose* and *Miranda Rites*. His goal is not to debunk history, but to broaden the point of view on a certain subject.

Houston's admiration of the work of playwright and director George Wolfe (*The Colored Museum*), and experiences with theatre on both U.S. coasts, sparked his taste for satire. Like Wolfe, he avoids making his criticism didactic by clothing it in humor. He says, "Humor is a seductive device to pull people in, because everyone loves a laugh."[6] He frequently uses what he calls "emblematic" characters; characters that people know, who already exist in the minds of his audience members. Then, with large doses of irony, he sheds more light on them.

In addition, the nontraditional satirical style of Sterling Houston links him to playwrights Adrienne Kennedy (*Funnyhouse of a Negro*) and Suzan Lori Parks (*TopDog Underdog, The America Play*), although his work is less nightmarish than Kennedy's and less metaphoric than Kennedy's and Parks'. What is akin in their works is the play on/with history, the de-familiarizing of the familiar, and targeting/blasting stereotypical images. As in the plays of Sam Shepard, who worked with the Magic Theatre in San Francisco while Houston was in town, few Houston plays are without music. Also, most of Houston's works, like Shepard's, play better in an intimate theatre. Both are "products," or as Bigsby says of Shepard, "inventions" of the sixties with a love for movies and rock and roll.[7] Both are men with divided loyalties—musicians, actors, and writers—with all three artistic talents informing one another. While in San Francisco, Sterling Houston played with a band called the Fleshtones, an eclectic, theatrical, mixed-race group. After this group broke up he went on to play with the Spades, an all-black power rock band, before moving on to the Magic Theatre Company.

In this volume, the plays illuminate historical characters (Sam Houston), mythical larger-than-life icons (Osiris), infamous women (Martha Mitchell), and women facing the vicissitudes of life and their own demons (Lily Mae). Although Houston's plays are rooted in their historical context, history is a myth to revisit. They are rooted in the politics of our time, but also politics revealed through the ranting of a controversial, hallucinogenic hospital patient (Martha in *Miranda Rites*). He looks at racism, but racism as revealed through an unhealthy, interdependent relationship (*Black Lily and White Lily*).

The message unfolds most often in Houston's canon in the genres of comedy, farce, tragicomedy, tragedy, and melodrama. Subject and theme determine the genre. Characters are frequently developed with the talents of particular company members in mind. *High Yello Rose* is historical farce and *Isis in Nubia*, melodramatic morality play, while *Black Lily and White Lily* is domestic farce, and *Miranda Rites*, surrealistic tragicomedy. With the exception of *Black Lily and White Lily*, the plays in this collection are two-act dramas with music.

High Yello Rose satirizes the legend of the Texas revolution. Reviewer Robert Faires states, "Houston stuffs the larger-than-life figures of Lone Star lore into the theatre of the ridiculous, where all pretense to grandeur can be highlighted with clown white and scarlet lipstick."[8]

The Alamo, a historical landmark in San Antonio, Texas, is a constant reminder of the battle in which the Mexicans defeated the Texans, including Davy Crockett and Jim Bowie. The cry "Remember the Alamo" spurred the Texans as they rallied in pursuit of General Santa Anna, caught him off guard during a siesta, and defeated him at the Battle of San Jacinto. Emily Morgan, a mulatto bondswoman, the famous "Yellow Rose of Texas," distracted him and helped the Americans defeat him. Emily, now the subject of legend with a hotel named in her honor in downtown San Antonio, is the center of Houston's comic gaze at the famous historic characters of the revolution.

Houston caricatures Sam Houston, Santa Anna, and Davy Crockett in *High Yello Rose* with an all-female cast (cross-dressing). The women portray the characters from Texas history as egotistical, macho, libido-driven, braggart warriors. Casting the "heroic" males with women gave Houston a certain amount of freedom and flexibility to portray the male characters' viciousness and selfishness. "The eight-member, all-woman cast roars into the script with the fury of wild mustangs. . . . They mug it up to great effect, mocking the Lone Star legend with a dose of high melodrama that defuses bitterness and keeps it fun."[9] The women impersonating the men allow the audience to keep a certain distance and to see the piece in a different way.

The play is the reminiscence of Joe, an ex-slave, and Emily, a former bondswoman, whom he finds 30 years later in Philadelphia passing for a white aristocrat. Joe John Joshua is a composite of several slaves who were witnesses to the legend, although they were often left out. Joe and Emily travel back in their memories to their participation in the events of the conflict over the land. Houston highlights the importance of the land with one of his theme songs, "Love the Land," sung by both sides:

> I love the land,
> For los mountains and valleys,
> I'll fight to the death to defend,
> Till I'm the last standing man,
> . . .
> Please understand. . . .

Houston was inspired to write *High Yello Rose* by the response to a visit to the Alamo by Arnold Aprill, a Chicago director, Jump-Start guest director, and Houston collaborator and partner. Aprill noticed the lack of references to the Latinos who were on either side of the conflict and the emphasis on white heroism and "Manifest Destiny."

Houston wanted to explore the other side of the story, which he felt was a perspective that needed telling.

Like the Native Americans, Mexicans originally welcomed Americans to their land, even offering land grants if they converted to Catholicism and became naturalized citizens. If they married Mexican women they were given additional land. They could bring blacks with them, but not slaves. From their earliest immigration to Mexico, in large numbers by the 1840s, their overriding goal was to take the land for the U.S. They were driven by dreams of wealth and landownership generated by pamphlets and books from California. Many of these immigrants were illegal aliens, since Mexico had prohibited further immigration into Texas in 1830. By 1835, there were 20,000 American foreigners in Texas, greatly outnumbering the 4,000 Mexicans. Stephen Austin was part of this thrust to "Americanize" and take the territory for the U.S. The American insurrection against Mexico in 1836 started an ongoing conflict that led to Santa Anna ceding Texas, conflicts over the southern border, and finally Mexico signing the infamous Treaty of Guadalupe Hidalgo in which Mexico lost California, New Mexico, Nevada, and parts of Colorado, Arizona, and Utah in 1848. The aggression was driven by "Manifest Destiny" interpreted as the belief in Anglo-Saxon superiority.

Houston highlights the ignoble goals and the ignoble characters on both sides of the conflict between the Mexicans and the Americans. His drama is full of sexual bravado and piles of dead Mexicans on the floor because this was the reality in the conflict. American men bragged about how they were displaying their prowess in the Southwest not only on the battlefield but also in bed. Murder, robbery, and rape of mothers and daughters in the presence of tied-up males of the families were common along the Rio Grande. At the Alamo, 175 Texas rebels were slaughtered and many more executed at Goliad by Santa Anna; at San Jacinto, Sam Houston's army slaughtered 630 Mexicans—many in the act of trying to surrender. For many years later, the Texas Rangers had the reputation of killing Mexicans (and Indians) with a "take no prisoners" attitude.

Houston says of his rendition of the story, "It does not matter whether it is true or not; what is handed down is what is truth. Myth is truer than fact." In his view, the work is propaganda in that all history is propaganda. And in his view, the story needed to be told from the point of view of those left out of the glorious memorials: the unsung heroes and heroines.

The play has been a favorite in San Antonio and was featured at the ATHE (Association for Theatre in Higher Education) conference in 1998 in San Antonio. Many found it a welcome relief from the "stately sentiment" found in history books and movie renditions. Through the comic monologues, songs, dances, and bawdy business, reminiscent of classical comedy, Houston weaves a hilarious retelling of the legend that "barbecues sacred cows" and is entertaining and memorable.

Like *High Yello Rose,* the second play of the collection, *Isis in Nubia,* contains music and song. Houston's fascination with rewriting myth leads to a melodramatic piece that recounts the jealousy and treachery of Seth, Osiris' evil brother. In the play, the mystery and magic of the goddess Isis overcomes treachery. Houston's interpretation, as in the ancient myth, portrays the victory not only of life over death but also of good over evil. The ancient Egyptian myth of God/King Osiris, identified as the god of fertility and the god of the underworld, dates back to approximately 2400 B.C. Houston's drama is a tribute of a kind to the pre-Christian death and resurrection myth with its seasonal festivals including rituals celebrating Osiris' life and death.

Houston sets the *Isis in Nubia* story of faith, love, re-birth, betrayal, death, and transfiguration in ancient Nubia, south of Egypt "before the beginning, in the realm of dreams." Nubia, called the land of the Kush in the Bible, was the homeland of Africa's earliest culture with a history that can be traced back to 3800 B.C. His original concept for the piece was not Egyptian, hence Nubia as the setting. He wanted a black cast in traditional African dress with African dance and drumming. He wrote the piece at the height of his Afrocentric sensibility, and thus had a desire to Africanize the work, rather than Egyptianize it. His collaborators thought he was missing an opportunity for lush Egyptian costumes and settings, and thus, in production, the Egyptian concept replaced Houston's original vision. Houston hopes that some brilliant black company will do the play one day as a traditional West African piece, that is, without the Egyptian mystique.

Whether in Egypt or West Africa, the play's political message centers around the African/African American claim to Egyptian history. The play fuels the debate about the ethnicity of the kings and queens of Egypt. It rewrites the story of the culture with blacks at the center (not marginalized or left out), as Osiris, Seth, and Isis. It draws blacks in ancient Africa in glorious tones: revered and also beautiful, powerful, and mystical.

Houston juxtaposes attention to the serious details of the heroic story with his comic voice that finds expression frequently in seemingly contemporary stylistic modern dialogue and gestures. The love story between Isis and Osiris is especially poignant because of memorable songs and poetic language. The poetry of the love songs had a special meaning for Houston who was experiencing similar feelings in his own life at the time.

Isis, in production, is theatre with imaginative sets, enchanting music, and colorful exotic costumes. The scene changes from throne room to ballroom, nobleman's parlor, the ocean, and the banks of the Nile River with subtle changes in the arrangement of the set pieces. The drumming, rhythmic light changes, dance, dragons, and wizards, along with praise singing, and ceremonial choral chanting weave magical, theatrical pageantry.

The play was produced at the Carver Cultural Center in San Antonio (1994–95 season), one of the many collaborations of Jump-Start with the Carver, a theatre house that is the historic center of black cultural life on the East Side of San Antonio.

The third play, *Black Lily and White Lily*, is a domestic tragedy in four scenes. Set in San Antonio, Texas, the play's quiet surface hides a volatile rage. The interdependent relationship of Lily Winslow and her servant Lily Mae is outwardly cordial; however, hatred and betrayal are at the core. Lily Winslow has always been aware of Lily Mae's betrayal, but Lily Mae, in the course of the play, comes to a realization of the betrayal of her employer. Through revelations about her mother, Lily Winslow reveals her racial prejudice. Lily Mae's final comment to Lily Winslow throws into relief a hatred of her mistress that is finally and shockingly unleashed. Houston reveals a command of poignant dialogue with a rich subtext in Chekhovian style.

Though not apparent in the text, the play was a part of another piece, *Kool Jams 91*. The production was a mixed-media presentation that progressed in nonlinear fashion from one farcical vignette to another. The work was a series of monologues and duets; with each one the audience learns more about the characters, culminating in this embarrassing truth: in *Black Lily* it's betrayal.

In *Black Lily*, the mistress and maid watch T.V. together and share their reactions to the events displayed there. At one point a rap group comes on BET. As they watch, so does the audience; the television screen was visible to the audience. As a big screen projection on the scrim, it was the major visual design element.

Houston revels in the involvement of the audience in performances of *Black Lily*. He frequently tells the story of a woman in the audience who anticipates the final action of the play and calls for it verbally. The inspiration for the piece comes from Houston's own mother's experience working for white women in San Antonio. His mother broke from domestic work to develop a successful, independent travel agency.

Miranda Rites, the final play in the collection, shows Houston's work in the realm of the surreal. Martha Mitchell, Watergate scandal whistle-blower, is now sick and hallucinating in a hospital in 1974. The play is not so much about the Watergate scandal as it is about a strong ambitious woman who spoke out and was destroyed by those she supported. The parallel with Marilyn, Dorothy, and Carmen is that all had great ambition and success in common in male-dominated fields, and a vulnerability that was cruelly exploited by powerful men. The play exemplifies Houston's continuing fascination with the vulnerability and strength of women. The story of this play sparks Houston's interest in issues related to justice and the dispossession of the weak or powerless by the strong and powerful.

In *Miranda Rites,* Mitchell is deteriorating mentally as well as physically. The world of her mind is rich with the images of her past that collide and change with images of the doctors and nurses in the hospital. They are of other women who had connections to powerful men and died untimely deaths: Marilyn Monroe and Dorothy Dandridge. They function partially as empathetic confidantes for expressions of her frustrations with men, politics, and life in general. The second act ends with a failed final appeal to her husband, John Mitchell, the former Attorney General of the United States. Martha Mitchell is also visited by an angel of death in the persona of Carmen Miranda who has come to read Martha her rites: ironically, it is the right to remain silent.

The drama *Miranda Rites* plays with the notion that Martha, who is said to have died of a rare bone marrow cancer after being discredited by former friends and branded crazy by the media, was helped to untimely death because she knew too much and was too willing to talk. With glimpses of insanity and clarity, slowly Martha moves toward death in a colorful, musical, exotic dream world where the images materialize, collide, fade, and return.

From *High Yello Rose* to *Miranda Rites,* Sterling Houston shows versatility in creating characters that are comic, serious, tragic, absurd, good, and totally evil. The plays are not only compelling reading but also lively production pieces.

Sandra M. Mayo, Ph.D.
Director, Multicultural and Gender Studies
Associate Professor of Theatre
Texas State University
San Marcos, Texas

Notes

[1] Sterling Houston, interview by Sandra Mayo, tape recording, Jump-Start Performance Co., San Antonio, TX, June 2003.
[2] Ibid.
[3] Ibid.
[4] Ibid.
[5] "Mission Statement," San Francisco Mime Troupe, Website http://www.sfmt.org/mission.html, accessed December 2003.
[6] Houston Interview.
[7] C. W. E. Bigsby, *Modern American Drama: 1945–1990* (Cambridge, MA: Cambridge UP, 1992), 171.
[8] Robert Faires, rev. of *High Yello Rose, Austin Chronicle,* Sept. 1993.
[9] Ibid.

References

Bigsby, C.W.E. *Modern American Drama: 1945–1990.* Cambridge, MA: Cambridge UP, 1992.

Faires, Robert. Review of "High Yello Rose," *The Austin Chronicle,* Sept. 1993.

Houston, Sterling, interview by Sandra Mayo, tape recording, Jump-Start Performance Co, San Antonio, TX, June 2003.

Kaufman, David. *Ridiculous: The Theatrical Life and Times of Charles Ludlam.* New York: Applause Books, 2002.

The San Francisco Mime Troupe. " Mission Statement." Accessed 2003, http://www.sfmt.org/mission.html.

Takaki, Ronald. *A Different Mirror: A History of Multicultural America.* New York: Little Brown, 1993.

High Yello Rose

High Yello Rose
L-R: Katherine Griffith, Kim Corbin, and Veronica Gonzales
Photo by Jill Ann

High Yello Rose

(Una Legeñda Verdadera de la Revolucion de Tejas)
Written in collaboration with Arnold Aprill

High Yello Rose was first presented by Jump-Start Performance Company on April 27, 1992, with the following cast:

Gertrude E. Baker	Joe John Joshua
Deborah Basham	Eastern Lady, Texian Soldier
	Col. Morgan, Old Anglo Woman
Kim Corbin	Emily Morgan, David Crockett
Felice Garcia	Magdalena, Santanista Soldier
Veronica Gonzales	General Santa Anna
Katherine Griffith	General Sam Houston
Cathleen Pollock	Eastern Lady, Texian Soldier
Lisa Suarez	Concepcion, Miguelito, Santanista Soldier

Directed by Arnold Aprill and Sterling Houston
Production Design by Robert Rehm
Lighting Design by Max Parrilla

High Yello Rose was also presented in the fall of 1993 with the original cast at the Planet Theater in Austin, Texas. In August of 1998 a performance was commissioned by ATHE (Association of Theater in Higher Education) at Jump-Start Theater for its annual conference in San Antonio.

Characters:

EMILY	"High yellow" woman, indentured servant
SANTA ANNA	Middle-aged but still charismatic self-made emperor of Mexico
SAM HOUSTON	Enigmatic leader of the Texianistas
JOE JOHN JOSHUA	Slave, freed when master died at Alamo
TWO SANTANISTAS	Soldiers and soldaderas in SANTA ANNA's camp
TWO TEXIANISTAS	Americans determined to take Texas by force. "Texianistas" is used for its comic effect as it relates to "Santanistas," but there is no historical precedent for its use.
OTHERS	Old Woman, Ladies, Concepcion, Magdalena, David Crockett, James Bowie, Col. Morgan, Soldiers, etc.

Prologue

(*Lights up on* EMILY *and* TWO LADIES *who sit stiffly in a parlor.
They are all fiftyish and dressed for tea.*)

1ST LADY: My dear, these pastries are just scrumptious! I've never
tasted anything quite like them before, have you Hortense?

2ND LADY: Truly, no. In all my years of taking tea, these take the
cake. What do you call them?

EMILY: Empanadas. A Mexican delicacy.

1ST: Em-fa-NA-dias! How quaint. You are so fortunate to have Concepcion and Magdalena to cook, clean, and in general take care
of you and your husband in your twilight years . . .

EMILY: We are indeed, blessed.

2ND: . . . The servant problem here in Philadelphia is nothing short
of a scandal.

1ST: But that shall surely change now that General Lee has surrendered. We should soon be getting a flood of good reliable colored
help, anxious for honest work. (*Clock strikes.*) My, is that the
right time? Where does it go? Come, my dear; we must be off.
(THEY *rise.*)

2ND: Thank you for tea, my dear. It was quite refined.

1ST: Don't you be a stranger Emily. You must come visit us soon.
(LADIES *exit.*) (EMILY *rises and turns on music box. It plays a
"pop" version of the "Yellow Rose of Texas" theme.* EMILY *does
a stiff little dance.* CONCEPCION *and* MAGDALENA *rush in.*)

CON.: Mrs.! Mrs.! He's back again!

MAG.: He won't go away! We told him to go, pero he won't go!

CON.: He says he's the best knife sharpener in the world, and he
won't leave till he sharpens yours!

MAG.: He's crazy; he says he knows you, Mrs.

EMILY: Knows me?

CON.: Sí! Knows you from long ago. (*Stage whispers*) In TEXAS!

EMILY: You know you are forbidden to speak that word in my presence. Remember your promise, or I'll not hesitate to send you
back where you came from.

MAG.: Pues, that was almost thirty years ago. Everybody's forgotten
about it already.

CON.: Everybody but you.

EMILY: You are wrong. I have forgotten, too. Do not remind me!

(JOE *bursts in. The women gasp.*)

JOE: That's my music. How did you get my music out of my heart
and into a music box without me knowing about it?

CON.: You are confused Mr., eh, . . . Mr. . . .

JOE: Joe. Joe John . . .

EMILY: Joe John Joshua? I can't believe it!

MAG.: You are confused Mr. Joe John Joshua.

CON.: This is a commercial music box, direct from New York City.

MAG.: . . . And Mrs. has never been to Texas.

BOTH: Never! We promise.

EMILY: . . . although the song you hear does have Texas in the title . . . Perhaps my knives and scissors do need a bit of sharpening. Maggie, Connie, will you fetch them please? I will speak to this fellow.

BOTH : Yes, Mrs.! *(They exit giggling.)*

JOE: *(Closes music box.)* I wrote that song! I wrote it for you when you were Emily Morgan before you became what you are now. It was my song all right, but sounds like somebody took it away.

EMILY: But how can music be stolen? I never realized . . .

JOE: Anything can get stolen around here, from the looks of it. Else, how could you stomach yourself passing for a white lady?

EMILY: Joe, don't! You don't understand. You never did. I have had the life I wanted. Why shouldn't I have a respectable place in the world without being looked at like I was part monkey woman?

JOE: You are a respected woman now, is that it? But, what about respecting yourself?

EMILY: I don't need self-respect! I need to be able to breathe deeply without choking on the fumes of my own bitterness.

JOE: *(Whistles)* That there Ethiopian blood must be some powerful stuff. If the few drops it took to turn your white skin yellow are enough to transform your European heart.

(MAG. *and* CON. *enter arguing in Spanish, and carrying knives to be sharpened.)*

CON.: No! 'Ta loca¡ No creo Santa Anna tienen más grandes huevos que Sam Houston! No way, José.

MAG.: Pues, creo que sí; pero, you think you know toda la 411.

CON.: Tell her, señora, that General Sam Houston was the bravest most macho general in La Revolution de Tejas . . .

MAG.: No way! El hombre número uno se fue General Antonio Lopez de Santa Anna, the Napoleon of the West, no less.

CON.: In your dreams, mija. Tell her, Mrs. You know the truth of it, verdad?

EMILY: I don't know what you mean. I must never speak of those times. . . . I have forgotten myself.

JOE: Then, I will tell it!

MAG. & CON.: YOU?!

JOE: I will tell it all. 'Cause I was there from the beginning, and I remember everything. Fact is, the whole thing started cause of me, if you want to know the truth. You see, that slave-owning, horse thief President Andrew Jackson, had his mind made up on Texas. He wanted it bad, for the riches and prestige it would bring him. Wanted it bad enough to kill for it, so he sent in a few of his hand-picked special agents to initiate covert actions against the Mexican people.

CON.: I don't believe it!

JOE: Covert actions which led eventually to the overthrow of the sovereign government of Mexico . . .

MAG.: Tell it like it is, mi hermano negro . . .!

EMILY: Must you talk of these things, Joe? Let them have their myth of heroes.

CON.: Yeah! It's all we got.

JOE: I care not to take your story away, but to tell my own. I am an old man who remembers everything. I especially remember you, Emily, meeting you in the chaos of revolution.

EMILY: But first a little background. Music, professor!

(TEXIANISTAS *sing*)

O Sam Houston where are you?
Your nation needs you today!
Mexico's taking back Texas
El Paso to Galveston Bay,
Coahuila to Colorado,
The story that has to be told
Santa Anna's taking back Texas
At the battle of El Alamo.

ACT ONE
Scene I

(SAM *sits isolated in light.*)

SAM: Howdy. I'm Sam Houston. Freedom Fighter; agent of change. I'll be president some day just you wait. But you know, that slavery thing. It really bothers me. Deep in my heart it rattles and aches. The Mexican government had sense enough to outlaw it outright. But, there's still a brisk business 'round here in indentured servants with ninety-nine-year leases. There's been many a black man I'd sooner have beside me in a close fight than quite a number of my own Anglo-Saxon race. Anybody who ever read the classics as I have, would recognize that the African possesses an old soul, with deep roots in the Cosmos. I understand. It's simple economics. They were built to withstand long hours working in the hellish sun, and somebody has to get the crops in. Folks in Europe are going naked for want of American Cotton. Economics, pure and simple. That, and an insatiable greed for adventure, greater even than the lust for land. In my formative years, you see, I lived among the Cherokee people, to live among them is to respect their ways. I am fortunately graced by an acquaintanceship with more than one way of life. *(Raises hand "Indian style")* Howdy! I'm UtseTi Aretaski. That's my Indian name; means "Big Drunk." Not that I could do anything about it, of course. Slavery, I mean. After all I'm only one man, and my instincts tell me that now is not the time to take a stand on that little issue. Still, it bothers the hell out of me. I swear to God. *(A pair of buckskin-clad bumpkins wander in.)* But meanwhile, duty calls . . . *(To men)* Howdy!

1ST: Howdy.

2ND: How, do.

SAM: Where're you boys from?

1ST: Kentucky and Alabama.

2ND: Louisiana and Tennessee.

SAM: And you come to Texas soon as you heard about it, I bet.

1ST: Dang right! Heard there was cheap land, loose laws, and purty senoritas.

2ND: That's my recipe for happiness, might near.

SAM: How'd you boys like to come with me and kick Santa Anna's ass? If we win, there's free land for the taking, and all the tail you can trim.

1ST: Santa Anna? Sounds like a Mexican to me. Let's go get him.

2ND: Sounds good, but ain't that a breech of international law? He's the president of Mexico, and Texas is still IN Mexico, strictly speaking.

SAM: Son, we owe it to Texas to take her away from the Mexicans. He'll never figure out what to do with her. We need her and she needs us. We got people coming. More and more every day . . . We outnumber the native-born round here two to one already. My orders are coming from someone much higher than myself.

1ST: God Almighty?

SAM: No. Andy Jackson. President Jackson wants Texas, needs it like a drunk needs whisky, and by God, I'm gonna get it for him, if I have to kill every little brown person between here and the deep blue sea! Are you with me, boys? For Freedom and Free Land!?

1ST: Count me in!

2ND: Me too. Let me at 'em!

SAM: Texas! Sweet Texas! Lying with her legs spread wide like La Chingada, wet and waiting for those big colonial cojones! Texas so like a woman, giving freely of her bounty sometimes, but other times, in need of a little coaxing . . . *(All three mount "horses" and begin to mime riding which turns into humping.)* Texas! I'm coming for ya! The Spaniards grabbed her; the French kissed her; the Mexicans took her, and now, it's MY turn!!

(All three let out sigh of satisfaction as lights go to out.)

Scene 2

(Streets of San Antonio. DAVID CROCKETT walks up to two Tex. soldiers)

DAVID CROCKETT: Can one of you boys tell me where I might find General Samuel Houston?

2ND SOLD.: Ol' Sam's out east with his army trying to hold on to Texas . . .

DAV.: Tell him Colonel Crockett has arrived and his troubles are just about over.

1ST SOLD.: You ain't no Davy Crockett!

2ND SOLD.: If you're Davy Crockett, I'm John Wayne and this here's my sidekick Andy Divine!

1ST: Everybody knows that ol' Davy always sports a coonskin-tail hat and a fringy buckskin suit!

DAV.: No, no, that was Daniel Boone, you ignorant fellow. History will forever confuse me with that lucky bumpkin. I am not "Davy," but DAVID Crockett. I have never sported a coonskin, and in fact, all fur makes me sneeze up a storm. As for buckskin, I love what Ralph Lauren has done with it this year, but I prefer for myself, a nice cut-away gabardine.

2ND: Well, I don't know . . .

DAV.: I promise you that I am Colonel David Crockett, former U.S. Congressman, raconteur, fearless Indian killer, and a runaway slave's worse nightmare. I've come, like you I suppose, to kill a few little Mexicans in the name of American economic policy.

1ST: If you're really Davy Crockett, how old was you when you kilt your first bear?

DAV.: Only three.

2ND: What was your major accomplishment in Congress?

DAV.: I patched up the crack in the Liberty Bell.

1ST: By, God it IS you!

2ND: Hot Damn, Davy! I'm your Tennessee homeboy too!

DAV.: Listen boys, I hope you've learned something from this. I am not "DAVY." I am not my image. I am David. An image is a thing, like a movie star's persona. Mixing me up with the other is quite dangerous. It reminds me of the story of . . .

1ST: Sam Houston's army's all full up. You'll have to settle for Travis, Bowie, and the Alamo fort. We could sure use another martyr for white supremacy.

2ND: 'Specially such a famous one. Everybody's heard of YOU. Seen your plays . . .

1ST: Read your books . . .

2ND: Colonel Travis will be SO impressed.

1ST: Talk about your effete snobs . . . But he is a plucky little devil, I'll give him that.

2ND: Colonel Bowie's too sick to command. They say it's consumption . . .

1ST: . . . But knowing his ways, it's more likely syphilis.

2ND: He's in a sick-room with his curandera.

1ST: She might as well give him last rites, I expect.

DAV.: Take me to him, before it's too late!

2ND: Sure thing, Davy; but would you do us a favor and put this on. *(Hands DAV. coonskin cap.)* . . . Just so there'll be no embarrassing questions . . .

1ST: Yeah.

(DAV. takes hat, starts to put it on, then throws it down and jumps up and down on it.)

Scene 3

("Love the Land" theme, instrumental. After the battle, two SAN-TANISTA soldiers stack "bodies" of Alamo heroes into pile for burning.)

1ST: Pinché cabrones! How come we get all the shit detail? First it was grinding the masa for El Presidente's tortillas, and now . . .

2ND: Now we have to clean these stupid dead heroes of the Alamo. If it wasn't so hot around here, I might desert.

1ST: De veras, hombre. Where you from, bato?

2ND: Querétaro; eva un campesino. Chinga el sorteo!

1ST: Soy de San Luis. They drafted my ass, tambien. It was my cumpleaños, y todos la familia, y los gentes locales bebemos en la cantina. We got muy pedo. Next thing I knew, I was in the army, dude.

2ND: Orale tambien, and marching a thousand miles to kill los norteamericano invaders. Why don't they just go back where they came from, if they don't like it here in Mexico?

1ST: Verdad! We didn't tell them to come to this chinga place. Why do they want to, anyway? It's too pinche hot.

2ND: You said it!

1ST: They'll never amount to anything until they get some climate control. Tengo muy sed.

2ND: . . . And these pinche heroes smell bad, even for Gringos. *(An OLD WOMAN enters.)*

O.W.: What are you all doing? Stacking up those heroes like cordwood! You ought to be ashamed! These boys deserve a Christian burial.

1ST: Look lady, we've got orders to burn 'em.

2ND: That's the fate of dead traitors. At least it keeps the buzzards away, que no?

O.W.: Savages! You'll burn in hell for this blasphemy.

2ND: De veras, vieja, but hell ain't no worse than South Texas! *(O.W. exits.)*

1ST: A raspa would really hit the spot right now.

2ND: Sorry, hombre; you're about a hundred and fifty years too early!

(Lights dim, cross-fade to SANTA ANNA's tent.)

*(*TEXIANISTAS *sing)*

O Sam Houston where are you?
Your nation needs you today!
Mexico's taking back Texas
El Paso to Galveston Bay,
Coahuila to Colorado,
The story that has to be told
Santa Anna's taking back Texas—
At the battle of El Alamo.

(Lights cross-fade to SANTA ANNA)

Scene 4

(SANTA ANNA has supper in his tent after the Battle of El Alamo.)

SANTA ANNA: Nothing like the scent of fresh blood to sharpen the

appetite. Nopalitos and Calabasa con javelina a la parrilla. All growing wild in this region. Is this not the garden of Eden? I love mi tierra bonita. And to think, amigo, these pinche Texianistas have the unmitigated arrogance to think they can steal our ancestral lands out from under us simply because God told them it was okay? What do they take us for? Indians? I will crush them. I have an army of ten thousand warriors thirsty for their gringo blood. I will strike at the heart of these audacious intruders with the savage might of my nation's fury. This Alamo business. This is nothing but small tamales, business as usual. Swatting mosquitoes that mistake themselves for eagles. These bastards stung quite a number of my good soldiers too, including my barber. No quarter! Asked or given. Five or six survivors were brought before me, after I had told those pendejos over and over "no prisoners!" One of them was that woodsman, the Great Indian Fighter, como se yama, Davíd Crockéte. He demanded the mercy of an honorable death, claimed he was a congressman, as if that was a license to lawbreak! I ordered him shot on the spot. Beheaded and thrown on the pile with the other traitors. No quarter does not mean "con su permiso." Tomorrow we will head east and seek that upstart Sam Houston and his rebel outlaws. Miguelito! More wine! Do you want me to die of thirst in this hell hole?!
(SANTA ANNA *and* SANTANISTAS *sing*)
I love the land!
For los mountains and valleys
I'll fight to the death to defend
Till I'm the last standing man.
Me and the land.
And together we'll build us a nation
Where freedom takes power
And Justice alone takes command.

Please understand.
In the world of my dreaming made real
By the seemingly endless reserves of my will,
Free to kill to be free, free to kill to be free
To be sure it's all right, free to fight, free to kill,
It's all right!
If I have to, I'll happily hurt you
So try to stay out of my sight.

Please understand.
In the world of my dreaming made real
By the seemingly, endless reserves of my will,
Free to kill to be free, free to kill to be free
To be sure it's all right, free to fight, free to kill,
It's all right!
If I have to, I'll happily hurt you
So try to stay out of my sight.

Scene 5

(The home of COLONEL JAMES MORGAN, *wealthy patriot, ex-Northerner, and developer of Texas lands, at the mouth of the San Jacinto River. He sits at parlor table with* SAM.*)*

COL. MORGAN: Are you quite sure, Sam? Could there be some mistake in communication?

SAM: None, Colonel Morgan. We have spies. He's headed this way, all right. Heading for me and my army. Should be to Morgan's Point by sundown day after tomorrow. You just have the bad luck to be between us and him, and I guarantee you he'll want to stop by to pick up a souvenir or two.

COL.: I will advise the servants to begin packing. Surely, he will not harm our womenfolk, for I hear he has the disposition of a gentleman.

SAM: Do not be swayed by his love of lace and silver chamber pots, for he is as cold a killer as the greatest Roman general, cold and driven by relentless demons. His history is muddied by many contradictions.

COL.: Don't tell me you believe that story about the squaw and the patriarch of the greatest family in Kentucky? That this same Santa Anna is the bastard offspring of that cursed union?

SAM: This is Texas, Colonel Morgan. We've come to expect the unusual. And sure you know, sir, that one of my wives is a full Cherokee.

COL.: Sam, I meant you no disrespect.

SAM: The best years of my life were spent among her people. They have a sure fine notion of the important things in this world.

COL.: Pray, why did you leave this paradise?

SAM: Figured I better get out among my own and do what I could to keep the white man's guns from wiping out their nation . . . Do you read much, Colonel? History? Philosophy?

COL.: Not much time for that sort of thing with a wife and two daughters growing more troublesome with each day; and after all, we are a working farm and ranch with over 100 animals, 17 slaves, eh servants; indentured servants in the fields and 10 in the household, so not only am I husband, father, and lord of the manor, I am the chief of a small village with the health and welfare of every living creature on my head.

SAM: When you read the history of the world, Colonel Morgan, the nature of things as they are between the lines, it really makes you stop and think. Whether Santa Anna is a Spanish noble, a peon, or the very son of Satan, he has certainly put the fear of God in these Texian Freedom Fighters. He's cut off our supplies, out maneuvered our re-enforcements, and killed some of our finest young boys, without showing mercy for their tender years or their mothers' breaking hearts. And on top of that, he has the shamelessness to go about looking like a durn Paris dandy astride a white horse.

(EMILY *enters with serving tray. She and* SAM *stare at each other for a moment before she remembers her duty and places glasses on tray.*)

COL.: Thank you, Emily. Oh Sam, have you not had the pleasure of meeting . . .

SAM: . . . your young daughter! I see the favor in her . . .

COL.: *(Interrupting)* My servant, Emily, an indentured bondswoman, from far away New York.

SAM: . . . Beg your pardon.

EMILY: General Houston. I am honored to meet so legendary a warrior for justice.

COL.: Your reputation as an opponent of slavery has preceded you, Sam.

SAM: Miss Emily, such a heartfelt compliment from so charming a lady is a double joy. I am pleased you share my convictions that Texas remains a free territory.

EMILY: I am a free-born mulatto woman, sir, never chained nor whipped. But in a land of slaves, I am merely one more for the shackles.

SAM: What a crime against mankind to have you locked in bondage.

EMILY: And so it is, indeed for the least of us. Is that all Colonel Morgan?

COL.: Yes, thank you my dear. (*She goes.*) As you see, she has quite a mind of her own. We treat her like one of the family. My girls adore her.

SAM: I can sure see why. The hour grows late. I must get back to my men; we expect news from Travis at any time. (*Aside*) For those of you who are trying to follow the story. You and yours, Colonel, need to pack-up and git.

COL.: Godspeed you Sam! We'll send our food and useful goods to your camp.

SAM: Thank you, sir; and watch out for that rascal Santa Anna. He's a sly fox. (*Lights down*)

Scene 6

(*Cross-fade to* SANTA ANNA *on the road to San Jacinto. He is riding his white horse, eating opium, and talking aloud to himself.*)

SANTA ANNA: These rustics dare to make a monster out of me! These low bumpkins have the balls to cast me as the barbarian of the piece, when it is they that have so grossly abused our gracious hospitality by trying to steal the land on which they have been allowed to live as naturalized citizens. We treated them like guests. Don't talk to me about boorish behavior! I'm tired of these arrogant shits. No quarter! Kill all of them con gusto and then piss on their corpses. Throw them in a pile and burn them like the carcasses of diseased cattle! I am the leader of a Great Nation that swarms with angry people. They are angry with themselves; they are angry with me. But most of all, they are angry with this gang of land-grabbing Anglo-Saxon invaders carrying on like backwoods conquistadors! No quarter! None! I want all of them dead before me. Except for the women and children, of course. And the blacks. Those who wish to be patriots may join my army. Let the others run free to warn their former masters that Santa Anna is coming with his beautiful army, and he has not had a woman in three days!

Scene 7

(EMILY *and* JOE *are packing supplies and preparing to vacate Morgan's Point.*)

EMILY: That should be the last of it. Hurry Joe; help me with these candlesticks. Poor Mrs. Morgan was in such a mad rush. I know she didn't mean to leave them.

JOE: I'm hurrying Miss Emily. I don't want to meet up with that devil again this side of hell.

EMILY: Not "Miss." I'm just Emily. You're a freedman now Joe. Besides, I'm just as black as you, for all my golden skin.

JOE: Sorry, Mi . . . Emily. I forgot you ain't no white lady.
EMILY: Please, Joe; I shall never bear that burden. How did James
Bowie treat you? Did he make you sharpen his knife?
JOE: That's in the past. Dead like him. Right now, I cain't think of
nothing but the future, and how to make sure you're part of
mine.
EMILY: How downright courtly of you. But this is not the time for us,
is it? Don't you sense that? *(They embrace and kiss.)*
JOE: *(Shouts and shooting off)* MY GOD in the morning!
EMILY: Let's run for our lives! They're killing everybody! (SANTAN-
ISTA *soldiers burst in with drawn swords.)* Have mercy!
1ST SOLD.: Do not worry my paloma. El Presidente does not kill
contraband persons. And you will be a welcome captive. I might
even get promoted to sarge. Move out! *(Exit at swordpoint.* 2ND
SOLDIER *gathers up candlesticks and other loot. Lights out.)*
*(Song: "High Yellow Rose" theme, instrumental—"Yellow Rose of
Texas")*

Scene 8
(JOE *is alone in a POW tent, a guard returns with* EMILY.)
JOE: You O.K.? He didn't mess with you, did he?
EMILY: I'm fine. He wants to have dinner with me.
JOE: He wants to have YOU for dinner.
EMILY: But can he stomach such a salty dish?
JOE: Why you talk like that? You know it drives me crazy! *(He
clumsily nuzzles her.)*
EMILY: No time for that stuff now; we got plenty to do before to-
morrow. I bribed a soldier to leave a horse for you tied on the
eastern edge of the bivouac. Ride him as fast as you can to Sam
Houston's camp. He's in the river bend, about eight miles past
Morgan's Point. Think you can find it?
JOE: Sure I can.
EMILY: Good. Give him this map. It tells him exactly where we are,
and how many there are here. Tell him all is well and in God's
hands. I will preoccupy the General as best I can till he can get
here.
JOE: You want me to leave you here alone with Santa Anna! I can't
do that.
EMILY: You can and you must, Joe. Nothing less than the future of
Texas rides with you.
JOE: I'll be back before tomorrow night has come.

EMILY: I hope you will, and have Sam Houston with you. I told Santa Anna that Houston was about three hundred miles north. He won't be ready for battle for days.

JOE: I'll ride like the wind. So long.

JOE: (*Riding to* SAM's *camp that night. Music under.*) I'm Joe. I'm John. Sometimes I'm Joshua, too. They all inside me. Probably more. I escaped death and became a free man fighting for slave Texas. Jim Bowie bought me from the famous Jean Lafitte. Gave me this big ol' frog-sticker when he croaked. Travis made me come along so he could feel more the gentleman with a slave beside him fighting for his right to hold slaves. That was John talking. Hollywood showed him taking it in the back to shield his good master Jim Bowie from a Mexican bayonet. But he's here. Inside me. I'm Joshua now; I feel his young sap flowing like first love. You remember me? For how long. And I'm still Joe too, don't forget. If I could do what I WANT to do, I'd quick as lightening join the Santanistas, and when this war is over, high-tail it down the gulf coast of Mexico till I got to Vera Cruz. Vera Cruz! Just across the gulf from my Island cousins. We could start a fellowship of new world free black people. I would learn their rhythms, and I would teach them a more judicious use of spice. Together we would unite in triumph over the diaspora!! But just like Hollywood, I'll stay here and be the revolution's errand boy. Just so I can be near the one I love. I do love Emily, you know. Love her so much I'll go against my own better judgment to help her out. But ain't that what love's all about?

(Sings)

There's a yellow rose in Texas
My true love she will be
No other dark man knows her
No white man; only me
She's the sweetest rose of color
That the world shall ever know
Until the day I join her
My poor heart is full of woe.
You can talk about your Lily Mae
And sing of Rosa Lee.
But the High Yellow Rose of Texas
She's the one, dear one for me!
I love a coal-black woman
And a fancy fine fair brown;

But a fair, fine-hair high-yellow
Sure to get my damper down;
She's the queen of chocolate bayou,
She's honey from the bee;
She's the High Yellow Rose of Texas,
And together we'll be free.

Scene 9

(HOUSTON's *camp.* SAM *has just finished reading mail.* JOE *stands near.*)

SAM: You are a brave man, young Joe. With this intelligence, we might be able to catch ol' Santa Anna with his britches down. How is Miss Emily?

JOE: Emily is well enough. I can't wait to get her out of Texas—her and me both. No offense, sir.

SAM: None taken. Emily is my idea of a patriot. Self-sacrifice is her true nature. I don't blame you for wanting to go, however. Texas is inhabited by a heap of hard-headed hombres bound and determined to see you both in legal bondage. I'm again'it, but I'm only one man, and I learned long ago not to make long-term promises. Ask the Cherokee about promises. Utseti Arataski knows about promises.

SOLDIERS: You tell 'em Big Drunk.

SAM: I just want you to know that, in my book, both you and Emily are heroes of the revolution. That's a fact. It's a damn shame nobody will ever know about it.

JOE: I hear you, sir.

SAM: Grab yourself some grub, young Joe. We ride at dawn tomorrow. (JOE *exits*) What is there about this place, these people, that draws me heart and soul into their conflict? Andy Jackson, it's all your damn fault. There I was living a perfect full life, and Andy sent me down here to cogitate with the local Cherokees, a splendid people by the way, to make sure they didn't take sides with Santa Anna in this war, and by durn if I don't end up general of a revolutionary army. Must be pure fate. Those old Greeks believed in it sure enough, Homer, Odysseus. It's a handy explanation for the unexplainable. If fate would have it that my army of farmers and traveling rogues is to do battle with the mighty Santa Anna and his legions, then so be it. There's a lot of real estate hanging in the balance. What we lack in uniforms and fit victuals, we more than make up in our dogged determination to

live free to establish free enterprise or die trying. When it comes
right down to it . . .
(SAM *and* TEXIANISTAS *sing*)
I love the land.
For its cotton, tobacco and sugar cane
Good grazing grain
Makes me feel good again.
Try to understand.
That a man needs his African labor
To plant in the summer
Tend to the children and
Harvest his land.
So I'll fight for the right to be free
Free to kill to be free
Free to fight when I'm right
In God's sight!
Free to kill, it's all right.
In the wisdom of God we all trust
'Cause he's a White Man like us!
(*Lights out*)

END OF ACT ONE

ACT TWO
Scene I

(*The following afternoon. SANTA ANNA and EMILY in his tent. Candlelight and fine fixtures in a luxurious setting. SANT. is dressed in white silks under a velvet dressing gown decorated with medals. EMILY is in a fancy "captured" dress and jewelry.*)

SANT.: Turn around slowly and let me examine you in detail. Ah
yes! You glow like a yellow rose in the moonlight. God has heard
my prayers.

EMILY: More champagne, señor? More tamales? (*She serves him.*)

SANT.: Do you think me a clown? A fool?

EMILY: No, Excellency! One does not become Emperor of Mexico by
accident. You have surely earned the title.

SANT.: As sanguine as you are beauteous, my blossom.

EMILY: Do you flatter all your prisoners so?

SANT.: Only those who dare to take my heart prisoner. Stop serving
me. Come. Come sit beside me. I want to kiss your lips. I want
to taste you. (*She sits and they kiss.*)

EMILY: Well?

SANT: Like honeysuckle and rose over an open flame. (*They kiss more passionately.*) Here in this tent, there is no world but the world we make. You are no longer a slave, a servant. You are a woman here by her own will. Why do you smile such a smile?

EMILY: Forgive me, but it is so odd to find myself here making love to the enemy general among the finery of my former life.

SANT.: You have shed no tears for your slain masters? Are you thus coldhearted?

EMILY: My tears are for the living.

SANT.: You are a woman like no other. I confess; I have not known the tender companionship of your sex for more than three days. For a voluptuary like myself, this is an eternity! And you are a rich capriotada for the breaking of so long a fast . . .

EMILY: You are no celibate. I have seen the soldaderas in your camp. I've listened to them giving relief to your battle-happy soldiers.

SANT.: Oh they are very well for my army, but I never touch them. They are crawling with lice. I have awaited your capture.

EMILY: They are no doubt true, the things that they say about you. . .

SANT.: What things? I am always interested in what pretty women say about me.

EMILY: All manner of things, Excellency . . .

SANT.: Tell me, dammit. Such talk causes my sap to rise.

EMILY: Well, Excellency . . .

SANT.: Toñio. Please call me Toñio, querida.

EMILY: Well, Toñio, they say you are richer than George Washington and possess the spirit of the fighting bull between your strong legs . . .

SANT.: The BULL? I prefer to compare my passion to the graceful brutality of the mountain lion. The Sacred Jaguar of Aztlan!

EMILY: Some say that you are not even Mexicano, but a half-breed adventurer from Kentuck.

SANT.: Bah! I have heard these stories. That I went to West Point, that I was half Indian! How could both be true? I hate Indians. The only thing I hate worse than Indians is white people!

EMILY: We can no more properly call them "Indians" Toñio. Indeed, this land is not India.

SANT.: De veras, Rosa mio. They should be called Americans, for is this not their homeplace? These Anglos won't even admit to Columbus' errors in judgment. How can they be expected to address their own? Do you like silk, my dove of the arroyos?

EMILY: Yes, of course. It's like heaven.

SANT.: So do I, my dear, so do I. I like it better than anything except the sight of my enemy's blood. Come, feel my silk shirt. Yes. Touch my silk underpants, they hold a stiff arrow aimed at your sweet target . . . *(Lights out)*

Scene 2

(That afternoon. Two SANT. guards stand before the closed tent. Noises come from inside.)

SANT. *(From within)* Rosa! Mi Rosa!!

EMILY: X-X- Excellency! Excellenceeeee!

1ST SANT.: How long can they go on like that?

2ND SANT.: It's disgusting, no? I can't even hear myself think. *(Noises, shouts within)*

1ST SANT.: It's too hot to be doin' the nasty.

2ND SANT.: Somebody better tell the Generalissimo. Has he got los grandes cojones, or what, bato? *(More noise within)*

1ST SANT: It they don't stop pretty soon, I'm going to have to find me a ruca. Why should we be the only two pendejos not enjoying ourselves.

2ND SANT.: You're right, Carnal; everybody's either sleeping or getting busy.

1ST SANT.: It's too hot to fight anyway.

2ND SANT.: Hell, let's go join the fiesta! He'll never miss us!

1ST SANT.: Vamanos! Ha! Ha! *(They exit.)*

SANTA ANNA: My dam is breaking again; it's about to flood your valley!

EMILY: Hold on one more momento, my bull of the mountains; my storm clouds are almost ready to release their rain . . .!

(Shouts off: "Remember the Alamo!!" "Remember Goliad! "Remember Pearl Harbor!" "Me no Alamo!" "Me no Pearl Harbor!!!")

SANT.: *(Coming out of tent)* What th . . . Holy shit! *(Shouts: The enemy is come! Run for your lives!)* You! You have done this Emily! *(He tries to dress.)* How could you? You have deliberately delayed your climax in order to give Sam Houston more time to advance!

EMILY: *(Comes out of tent)* It's better this way, Toñio . . .

SANT.: I am General Antonio Lopez de Santa Anna! Emperor of All Mexico! Napoleon of the West! It is not my destiny to die here today in the company of a spying whore. If I had more time, I'd

kill you. Adios, puta! As long as the prickly pear blooms this land will forever be MEXICO . . .! Because . . .
(Sings) I Love the Land . . .! *(Shouts of "Remember the Alamo" as he runs off)*
EMILY: So like a man, to leave a lady lacking. *(TEXIANISTAS and SAM enter)* SAM!
SAM: Emily Morgan. We meet again.
EMILY: Did you catch the General? He ran off that way.
SAM: We'll take him in due time. I, and all the freedom-loving people of Texas, owe you a debt, Emily. We took them in a rout, thanks to the distraction you provided.
EMILY: I did it in the hope that the Morgan family will once again inhabit Morgan's Point. And in gratitude, I may be granted free passport back north.
SAM: If there be any favor, large or small that I may do, count it done.
EMILY: Perhaps. Perhaps one. We shall see how small it turns out to be . . . *(She leads him back into tent.)*
(SANTANISTAS *sing*)
O Santa Anna where are you?
Your country needs you God knows
Sam Houston's taking our Texas
And taking sweet Emily Rose. . . .

Scene 3
(After the battle, two TEXIANISTA soldiers pick through the bodies of dead and dying Santanistas.)
1ST TEX.: We sure kilt a bunch of them buggers, by damn! How many you think there is?
2ND TEX.: Too damn many to bury, I know that for a fact.
1ST TEX.: You're right about that. This here ground's gonna stink like grease for a hundred years.
2ND TEX.: You think Mexicans have souls like regular folks?
1ST: I reckon the good ones must go to some Mexican-style heaven, full up with candles and purty statues.
2ND: Lookey there! A gold snuffbox!
1ST: By damn if it ain't! Better get all you can off 'em now, Brother, cause by tomorrow they'll be starting to smell like rotten tamale shit.
2ND: You're right about that, brother! *(Pulls out a pair of pliers.)*
1ST: What's them for, Brother?

2ND: I can get two-bits a piece for Mexican teeth! (*He yanks out teeth from corpse.*)

1ST: Brother, you are one crazy peckerwood!

(WOMAN *walks by with babe in arms and searches through bodies.*)

1ST: Lookit! Ain't that one right pretty señorita!

2ND: By golly, I could sure suck on that little chile bean.

(*They begin circling her and touching her body.*)

1ST: Ain't it queer how Mexican senoritas is fine and docile like as a spring-born pup . . .

2ND: And their men is such mongrel scum . . .

(*They grab her.*)

WOMAN: No!Por favor, no puedo! Yo no soy una soldadera, soy la esposa de un coronel muerto! Ay Dios! (*Both men rape her on top of corpses.*)

1ST: Remember the Alamo!

2ND: Relax and enjoy it!

WOMAN: No! (*She curses them in Spanish.*)

Scene 4

(JOE *in his cabin preparing to flee.*)

JOE: (*Sings*)

She's the sweetest rose of color,
You ever want to see.
She's the High Yellow Rose of Texas,
Gonna run away with me!

(*Speaks*) Yes, by gumption, I'm outta here at sundown, gonna meet up with Emily and me and my gal gonna head way way down south till we get to the Islands! Then we gonna open up ourselves a knife sharpening business. Together we gone hone happiness out of dull, rusty discontent. We gonna . . . (*A loud knock*) Who knocks yonder? (SANTA ANNA *enters*)

SANT.: Forgive me, but I find myself in a rather embarrassing situation. You see. I must have your clothes.

JOE: My clothes? These clothes I'm wearing?

SANT.: You may take mine. Except, of course, for my diamond-studded shirt.

JOE: I don't know . . .

SANT.: (*Pulls out pistol and points it at* JOE.) I'm afraid I must insist. I would hate to make a hole in the chest of a compadre . . .

JOE: (*Steps behind screen*) O.K., but I'm keeping my brogans . . .!

SANT.: I knew I could count on your good judgment. (*They begin to exchange clothes.*) You may not think so at this moment, my friend, but today is your lucky day. Now you can tell your grandchildren that you have swapped duds with The Napoleon of the West. Did you know it was I?

JOE: Sure. I saw you real clear after that Alamo mission fight. Guess I owe you a debt of thanks for killing everybody there and making me a free man as a result. But it don't seem right somehow.

SANT.: Ah yes! The Alamo. An inadequate, suicidal fortification, but an excellent tourist attraction in the making . . .

JOE: What'll you do now? High tail it down to Mexico City?

SANT.: I have a feeling I might not be "man of the hour" in la ciudad, if you know what I mean. As a result of Texas being stolen by Houston and his pirates, I have lost one-third of my nation's territory, turning thousands of my people into instant foreigners in the land of their birth! I'd do well to let things cool down a bit before returning to El Capital . . .

JOE: I hear the Islands are real nice this time of year. Balmy and calm; people of every color, good food! Rum! I'm going there with my woman! Just as soon as I tell her, wait and see!

SANT.: Women! *(Spits)* I'm through with them! For a while. It was a woman who has placed me in my present predicament—a yellow, spying beauty that used her charms on me to assist that traitorous felon Sam Houston in stealing my country from its rightful owners. With my superior numbers and skills at battle, he never would have taken me. Never! If only I had not been in afternoon delicto with La Rosa Amarilla!

JOE: Sounds to me like not the woman's blame, but your own lusty nature's.

SANT.: I must keep my senses sharpened to a fine point in order to operate at peak level. But what do you know about a man of destiny like myself. You, a humble sharpener of other people's knives . . .

JOE: My own, too, sometimes, notwithstanding.

SANT.: *(The exchange is complete. BOTH step from behind screens.)* The Islands, you say? Perhaps not so bad a haven for a while . . . Quien sabés? There now. Do I not make a convincing beggar?

JOE: Except for your diamond studs . . .

SANT.: Oh, yes. How's that now? Perhaps I should stoop my shoulders a bit more. And frown.

JOE: That's it. That's pitiful.

SANT.: No sacrifice of dignity is too great, in the name of patriotism. Bueños suretes, mon ami. *(Exits)*

Scene 5

(SAM *is sitting under an oak tree. His legs are extended and one of his feet is bandaged.* TEXIANISTAS *bring in* SANTA ANNA *at gunpoint.*)

SAM: Well General Santa Anna, as I live and breathe!

SANT.: General Sam Houston, as I hope to do, too.

(There is a stiff pause.)

SAM: Well, sientete, for land's sakes. I can't get up to shake your hand, though I'd damn well like to.

SANT.: You have been wounded.

SAM: It's a little nothing! Escopeta ball hit my Achilles tendon. It just means I'll never walk straight again, is all.

SANT.: It least it was not your balls, eh?

SAM: By damn, general, you are a pistol! Ha! Ha! Ha! Ouch!

SANT.: You are in pain. How sad.

SAM: You really don't know how sad. I've sworn off the hootch for the duration of this little war, and I ate the last of my opium yesterday morning. *(He sobs.)*

SANT.: Ah, my general, the gods of the East have smiled upon you! *(He produces stash from his pant leg.)* I managed to spirit away a plug or two for my intended escape.

SAM: Glory be to Goddamm! I'll feel like my old self again, thanks to the valiant enemy chief. *(He chews drug.)* Ummmm! I do like eating it, don't you? Smoking it is such a waste, with all due respect to my Chinese brothers, half of it goes up in smoke to stone the birds. Thanks, general.

SANT.: It is the least I can do for the Great General Houston, for you have captured The Napoleon of the West!

1ST TEX.: If he hadn't been crying so loud, we would'a never found him under that bridge, Sam.

2ND TEX.: I didn't know who he was . . .

1ST: Hell, I didn't either! But I knew he must be some damn body with them diamond fuckin' buttons all down his shirt front.

2ND: . . . Then we marched him here by the prisoners and they started hollering "Mira, mira! El Presidente!"

BOTH: El Presidente!!

SAM: That musta cooked your sauce, huh, general?

SANT.: What will you do with me? Remember I am the commander-in-chief of a sovereign nation with European allies.

SAM: Some of the boys want to lynch you from a cottonwood tree and use you for target practice . . .

SANT.: What a joker . . .!

SAM: But I think I'll take you up to Washington, and hook you up with Ol' Hickory.

SANT.: Tie me to a tree? Is this some strange Norte Americano ritual?

SAM: Andy Jackson. Andy Jackson the President of the United States of America. By losing so handily, you've added a great deal to the land he can now legally call his own.

SANT.: Oh yes! The President on the Jax Beer label! I admire his taste.

SAM: Bet he would surely love to display you in Congress. Let the press play it up big. He's running for re-election, you know. Conquered dictators are real vote-getters.

SANT.: I will have to have new uniforms, of course. (1ST TEX. *brings him clean uniform coat.*) And medals. You did manage to confiscate my medals, I hope.

(SAM *motions and* 2ND TEX. *produces a small chest. He gives it to* SANT.)

SANT.: Ah! *(He opens chest and holds up medal.)* They are like my children! This one was from the immortal campaign of 1813. How glorious it was! Blood and purple fire. I will gladly meet with your illustrious president, as his humble captive, if you will answer me one question. It has been bothering me for days now. That Alamo business? What in the world were they thinking? They seemed determined to be slaughtered. I was forced to oblige.

SAM: And they'll be holding that one against you for many years, Generalissimo . . .

SANT.: But they were begging for it! Like a child willing to test your patience with annoying behavior just to see how long it will take you to slap him.

SAM: I have children too; I hear you.

SANT.: I must confess, I needed a victory badly, so it couldn't have come at a better time. You do understand, no?

SAM: I do. I needed the loss, too. A massacre is a great motivator of men, you know. Besides, war is not for lily livers.

SANT.: Sir! I am no coward! I am strong and brave enough to withstand the bitter assault of that cruel word in order that I may survive to fulfill my destiny. For he who runs away assures himself of at least the possibility of a long life.

SAM: Hell, I hope you live to be a wrinkled old white-head. I'm a big fan of your country, you know. A nation of riches whose great-

est treasure is a strong determined people. I might rule it myself
someday, don't be surprised.

SANT.: I must admire your arrogance, señor, and your tolerance for
opium.

SAM: Pain's all but gone. Help me up, boys. *(He stands, assisted by
TEXIANISTAS.)* Yes sir, can't you just see me! Emperor of the
greatest nation in the civilized world stretching from Canada to
the Yucatan. If Andy Jackson backs me up, I could take Mexico
City with five thousand ruthless men. Don't worry. I'll appoint
you Ambassador to the Court of St. James.

SANT.: But London is so dreary.

SAM: After all, let's face it: you and I have more in common than
not. I figured it out a long time ago, Santa Anna ol' pal. Some
men were just born to take a leadership position.

(Lights change. An OLD WOMAN interrupts. She is Anglo and poor.)

OLD WOMAN: Sam Houston! Sam Houston!! You clean up these
Mexican corpses at once, you hear me?! This might be a battlefield to you but it happens to be my farm, and I'll not have it
polluted up with these durn dead stinking Mexicans!

SAM: Madame, I sympathize with your plight. But I have no men
for gravedigging. Besides which, my boys hate them worse than
they hate Indians.

OLD WOMAN: I've got planting to do! You expect me to plow them
under like dry cornstalks?!

SAM: Why not? They'll make excellent compost for your crop. It's
all a part of the great circle of life and death. In and out; in and
out . . .

O.W.: Ahaaaaaahwa!

(SANTA ANNA speaks to SAM.)

SANT.: Allow me to handle her, compadre, for I have had much experience subduing unruly citizens. Madame, have a care how
you address your betters, for you are here only by our grace!
You exist at our pleasure. So grand is our personal vision, that it
has the power to spin history's great wheel, or if we so desire, to
bring it to a grinding halt. Do you like silk? Come with me my
little cucaracha . . .

(They exit together. JOE enters running.)

JOE: General Sam! General Sam! She's gone! She left without so
much as a "so long I'll see you later." My Emily! Why did she do
it? Why?

SAM: There, there, Joe boy. That woman has plans that don't include any of us, I hazard.

JOE: But I love her! I can't help myself from doing it. *(Sobs)*

SAM: Come on, pull yourself back together in one piece . . .

JOE: It ain't right! I ought to get the woman! That's the way it should be this time. For me! After all my trials, am I again to end up with nothing?

SAM: You've still got your black skin . . .

JOE: Nothing but my black skin? My GOD! This world ain't nothing but an ongoing torture from the first time you breathe the air; 'cause the air you breathe is the only thing in your life not trying to kick you down . . .!

SAM: Don't speak so eloquently about your suffering, boy; you'll only perpetuate it.

JOE: I even made up a song about her. Made it up from my heart. Never got to sing it for her . . . Now I'll never sing it!

SAM: Sing it for me. Lord knows I could use a tune.

JOE: *(Sings)*
I love a coal black woman
And a fancy, fine fair-brown
But a fair, fine-hair high-yellow
Sure to get my damper down.
She's the queen of Chocolate Bayou
She's honey from the bee
She's the High Yellow Rose of Texas and
Together we'll be free . . .

(During song, actors "age" and change into Prologue costumes.)

SAM: I reckon that's about the end of my usefulness to this little operetta. From the looks of things, I'd say we were about ready to go back to real time, 1866. I was three years dead by then, so I'll just be moseying back to that great bye and bye. By the time this music ends, I gotta be gone so, see you over there . . . Oh! As for that little "cojones" question raised early on. Think about it. The right answer will come easy . . .

(SAM disappears. Music concludes.)

Epilogue

JOE: That's all of it. All I remember after thirty years of searching for you.

CON.: NOW do you believe me?

MAG.: Why should I? All that story did was make me homesick for mi tierra!

CON.: Let's go make some chicken mole. That always helps. (THEY go.)

EMILY: What will you do, now? Keep going door to door, sharpening the knives of strangers?

JOE: I'm leaving this country altogether, now that the war is over, I'm going down to the Islands like I always wanted.

EMILY: I am my own woman, and my husband's. That is unthinkable.

JOE: What is unthinkable is not that, but the thought of you wasting away here in this shadow of a life. Come. Reclaim yourself with me.

EMILY: You are such a mad fool! Where would we go? Traveling through a land that hates us both?

JOE: I got it all planned out. We'll book passage on a freighter headed down the Atlantic coast, traveling as servant and mistress, till we get to the Islands; I got plenty money saved up. There we can at last be together and be free.

EMILY: Poor Joe. Don't you know that slavery plagues these lands much like our own national sickness?

JOE: Not where we're bound to. A fabulous, free black African Island in the middle of the Colonial sea!

EMILY: Where is this paradise?

JOE: Beautiful Haiti! Free for over half a century, Uncle Sam wouldn't dare put his hands on Haiti!

EMILY: But what of my good name? What of my husband?

MAN OFFSTAGE: Emily! Come in here woman, and help me clean out my earwax!!

EMILY: I'll come with you, Joe. It couldn't be any worse than Philadelphia . . .

(COMPANY enters for FINALE and curtain call.)

SONG: (Tune of "O Sam Houston")

ALL: (Sing) Vaya con Dios, my darling! Adios, so long, fare thee well!

JOE: (Sings) Stay by my side in my memory . . .

EMILY: (Sings) Or stay at my four-star hotel!

ALL (Sing)

Thank you Emily Morgan, for telling your story to me,

You gave us a true understanding

Of what it means when we fight to be free!

(Lights dim to out)

THE END

High Yello Rose
L-R: Katherine Griffith, Kim Corbin, and Veronica Gonzales
Photo by Jill Ann

Isis in Nubia
L-R: Kitty Williams, T-Bow Gonzales, Michael Verdi
and Gertrude Baker
Photo by Gary M. Perkins

Isis in Nubia

Isis in Nubia

a tale of ancient Africa

Isis in Nubia was first presented on May 26, 1994, at the Carver Cultural Center, San Antonio, Texas, with the following cast:

Robert Aden	Malacandar, Wizard, Old Soldier
Gertrude E. Baker	Priestess, Ishtar, Nile Woman
Donald Bouldin	Priest, Hapsut, Young Soldier
Xavier Cerda	Young Soldier, Nubian Man
Kim Corbin	Nephthys, Nubian Girl
Kevin Evans	Praise Singer, Gilgamesh, Horus
T-Bow Gonzales	Osiris
Mak Hall	Seth
Allana X. Schulman	Weaver, Nile Woman
Cassandra Small	Isis
Michael Verdi	Anubis
Kitty Williams	Priestess, Kali, Nile Woman

Directed by Sterling Houston
Production Design by Robert Rehm
Costume Design by Kim Corbin
Lighting Design by Max Parilla and Steve Bailey

Characters:

SETH	God of Night, Revenge and Darkness, brother of Osiris
OSIRIS	God of the Dead, Fertility and Rebirth
ISIS	Goddess of Morning, Harvest, wife of Osiris
HORUS	Warrior God, son of Osiris and Isis
NEPHTHYS	Sister of Isis and Osiris and wife of Seth
ANUBIS	Son of Nephthys
ISHTAR	Queen of Syria
MALACANDER	King of Syria
HAPSUT	A General

PRIESTESS, WIZARD, ATTENDANTS, NOBLES, SOLDIERS, DRUMMERS, MUSICIANS, GODS, DEMI-GODS, WOMEN and MEN of NUBIA, etc.

Time: Before the Beginning
Place: The Realm of Dreams

ACT ONE
Scene I

(An empty stage is covered by low fog and soft light. A drum beat signals the beginning of the world as set pieces come into view. A group of PRIESTS *enters dressed in desert robes and hooded.)*

1ST PRIESTESS: Long ago, before the priests and the pharaohs, when the pyramids were but a dream in the mind of Ra, the great dark king Osiris ruled in Africa.

*(*OSIRIS *comes into view on set piece.)*

2ND: He was tall and slender so that his body fit lightly upon his eternal soul. On his head, he wore the lofty crown of Nubia, adorned with ostrich feathers, as light and beautiful as truth.

(Drums increase tempo.)

3RD: His braided beard fell down his chin onto his strong black chest, befitting the one whose fertility made life swell, even in the desert.

1ST: Wherever he stepped, water lilies blossomed.

2ND: His naked body from ankles to wrists was decorated in gold and precious stones like drops from a rainbow.

(Drums out)

ALL: This was Osiris who ruled.

3RD: Powerful and black! Great Osiris took the people from the ways of beasts, and taught them humanity. *(Harp music up.)*

1ST: He taught the world the cultivation of the fields, the care of the sacred herds.

2ND: Using music, and gentle persuasion, he transformed the earth into a proud golden universe!

(Harp out.)

3RD: But all were not content with this perfection . . .

(Cross-fade)

(A low drum sounds. At the top of a tall platform SETH *in royal regalia is lit by red lights. Below him smoke swirls in the bluish dark.)*

SETH: Pity the creature, goddess or bitch who scorns my affection. Lest she prefer the thistle to the wild rose, let her take heed. *(Sound of howling wind.)* Such winds do now blow through the desolate cave where once beat my heart, such howling winds do chase themselves like mad dogs chasing their own tails reaching the velocity of hurricanes! All pity and woe to the bitch or goddess who turns from the sun to embrace the icy moon. *(Wind increases)* Blow down! Blow you ill winds from the mighty void of Hathor! Reach reluctant Isis! Send her spinning in the dizzying spiral of your magnificent confusion!!

(SETH *laughs demonically as winds build.* Lights down on SETH *cross-fade with storm.* ISIS *dressed in white mourning robes is buffeted about by the storm. Others making their way are stopped by her.*)

ISIS: Excuse me, good sir, but have you seen my husband Osiris?

MAN: What? No time now, get to shelter! Don't be a fool!

ISIS: He's quite a tall man, wearing a tall crown . . .

WOMAN: I think she's mad with grief. Poor thing.

ISIS: You! Perhaps you have seen a strange Nubian in these parts.

WOMAN: You're the strangest we've seen in quite a while! Let me go to my children.

ISIS: I must find him! I know he is near! I know it! I . . . OH!

(*Debris is flying in the windstorm, a camel perhaps and a palm tree. One of these hits* ISIS *on the head. She swoons, and is helped by a well-dressed royal man and woman,* ISHTAR *and* MALACANDER *of Syria.*)

MAL.: Poor woman. Bring her to the palace at once. Get us out of this infernal wind.

(*Wind out. Royal Attendants lift* ISIS *and carry her to the Palace, lay her on a divan as* ISHTAR *and* MALACANDER *sit at her head.*)

ISIS: *(Waking)* What . . . has become of me?

ISHTAR: You are in our palace in the land of Syria. Your head took quite a bump.

MAL.: How do you feel, my child?

ISIS: Who are you?

MAL.: I am King Malacander, ruler of this realm.

ISIS: I have heard of you from afar!

ISHTAR: And I am Queen Ishtar. It was a lucky thing we came upon you.

ISIS: Yes thank you, or I would have surely perished.

MAL.: You have come quite far, from the look of you.

ISIS: I left my home long ago, in the year of the seven jackals. I have been searching since for my lost husband.

ISHTAR: And what a husband he must be that you would search the world for him.

ISIS: He is the balm of my soul.

MAL.: You suspect that he is somewhere in Syria?

ISIS: I follow my nose.

ISHTAR: Your nose?

ISIS: I follow the air that holds the fragrance of his skin. Like sandalwood and honey heated by starlight. It is pungent in the air of your country.

MAL.: I doubt that he is here. Such a man would be easily distinguished by his Aetheopian sail and boat, his Aetheopian chariot and horse.

ISIS: He travels not by boat, nor horse, nor chariot.

ISHTAR: What then, on foot? (ISIS *weeps.*) Oh dear, what did I say?

ISIS: My lord husband, my dear Osiris, was murdered by his evil brother and his coffin set adrift in the Nile. I am told it washed ashore quite north of here, but other than his scent I have found no trace . . . *(Sobs)*

MAL.: Oh you poor, poor thing. What a world we live in.

ISHTAR: How did such a thing come to be?

ISIS: It began long ago, on a day that was to be a joyous occasion. It was my husband's birthday, you see, so we had a few friends over for a little get-together, and everything went fine until . . .

Scene 2

(A party in progress. Various Gods, Goddesses, and creatures of myth are dancing, drinking, and making out.)

KALI: That Osiris can really throw a party, can't he? I've seen folks here I haven't seen in eons. Isn't that Gilgamesh over there? Gil! You old monster, how's the world treating you!

GIL.: Kali! You old goddess of destruction, you! Gimme five! This is some kinda shindig, ain't it!

KALI: Tell me about it! And looks like all the Gods are here too. Even a few demi-gods, for good measure.

GIL.: Hey, but somebody is missing. Brother Seth. I haven't seen him anywhere.

KALI: Maybe he's ashamed to show his face after last year. The way, he carried on . . . even Dionysus was scandalized.

GIL.: He was so drunk.

KALI: Hell, we were all drunk; that's no excuse for putting the big-time make on your brother's wife . . .

GIL.: Right out in the open . . .

KALI: Where everybody could see . . .

GIL.: Especially Osiris.

KALI: But he was cool.

GIL.: Never said a mumbling word.

KALI: To his wayward brother.

GIL.: Such a good man. Heart like a lion.

KALI: Not like Seth. Petty and cruel.

GIL.: It's been the same since they were children.

KALI: Whatever Osiris had, Seth always wanted.

GIL: Always schemed to get it, by hook or by crook.

KALI: With such a brother, I thank the gods that I was an only child!

GIL.: With a mother like yours, I wouldn't be so sure.

KALI: Don't talk about my mama . . .

(Fanfare. ISIS and OSIRIS enter in full regalia.)

ALL: All hail Isis and Osiris! Osiris and Isis, King and Queen of this world and of the other worlds!! *(Cheers)*

ISIS: Osiris! Husband of my heart, I celebrate the anniversary of the day you sprang from the center of creation! Bless those sweet fates who have brought you to my side!

(Cheers. Attendants bring in bright feathered birds on a tray.)

GIL.: Accept these humble gifts, my King, as an offering to the soul of Hathor, she who unites all gods and mortals.

KALI: May she bless your eternal honeymoon. *(They kiss, as all cheer and congratulate them. Drums begin "Osiris Praise Song" and dance.)*

(Sings)

When I was young, the world was younger than me,
Darkness and Shadow as far as the eye could see;
Out of the Darkness, there broke a silvery light!
That was Osiris! Coming down, coming down, coming down
To make everything all right!

Oooosiris! You are much younger than we!
Oooosiris! Show us the way to be free!
Oooosiris! Son of the Earth and the Sky;
Oooosiris! Show us the way how to live and the way
How to die!

(Dancing gets wild until SETH and two attendants enter in war-like stances. All fall silent.)

SETH: Please, your pardon noble friends. Don't let my entrance spoil a scene of such tender bliss. My brother's pleasure is next door to my own.

ISIS: Seth, our brother! You are always welcome in your brother's house.

SETH: And you, dear Isis, do you welcome me as well?

ISIS: You're just in time. The party's just getting started.

SETH: Then let me add my tribute to those already heaped at your royal feet, my quiet brother.

(Attendants bring in an elaborate gilt-painted sarcophagus. Others reply: "Glorious!" "Wondrous!" etc.)

SETH: It is quite simply the most beautiful sarcophagus ever fashioned in the entire history of creation. It assures its owner an eternity of peaceful perfection! Does it meet your standard, royal brother?

ISIS: Such an extravagant gift must have cost you a god's ransom.

SETH: Ah! My brother, silent as ever and content to let a woman speak for you. Tsk, tsk!

ISIS: If Seth had such a woman, such silence would most become him. My lord, your brother speaks to me from heart to heart. To the heartless it must seem indeed like silence. But his language is as clear to me as a newborn spring. *(OSIRIS smiles.)*

SETH: My Royal Brother grins. A sign, I hope, of his approval.

(OSIRIS crosses to the sarcophagus and examines it, with eye and hand; others are silent. When he reaches the carved face he stares into it, holding it in both his hands. He smiles broadly, turns to face SETH with outstretched arms.)

SETH: Praise the Gods! I'm happy you are pleased. But come the hour of your extinction, I hope that I have guessed well in my estimation of your measurements . . .

ISIS: I'm sure it is well fitted . . .

SETH: There is but one way to end all doubt, of course. Why don't you try it on for size . . .

ISIS: No, I had a dream about this!

SETH: . . . So that I may be sure it needs no further alterations . . . (SETH *opens the lid of the coffin, and gestures for* OSIRIS *to enter.* OSIRIS *smiles a reassuring smile at* ISIS, *and after a pause, steps into the box.)* Just as I thought! *(Slams lid shut.)* A perfect fit!! (ISIS *screams as henchmen nail down coffin lid, others scatter in confusion and fear.* ISIS *tries to open sealed lid. She is pulled away struggling, and overcome by grief, she is carried off.)* That's right! Run away, you drunken deities run and tell all you meet that heaven has a new king and that he has brought a new day of power and blood to this stagnant land!! Throw my damned brother into the Nile and let him be king of the fishes! A fit kingdom for one of his density. His domain and royal consort Isis are now mine forever! And Isis! If she should struggle in grief against my charms, let her. All the better! For her every anguished cry blows hot upon my passion. She'll give it up in the end. They always do.

(Lights down as SETH steps into OSIRIS' throne.)

Scene 3

(Syrian palace. MALACANDAR and ISHTAR sit listening to ISIS.)

ISIS: To think now of that dreadful day fills me with pain.

ISHTAR: You sad little thing.

ISIS: I fought his advances for as long as I could, then one day, I had my fill of it and so escaped to search the world for my lost love.

ISHTAR: Poor child, you must be very tired.

ISIS: Well, I . . .

MAL.: Why not stay a while with us my dear; for our sake as well as your own. You could recuperate from your journey and help us with our young son, as well. We are a little shorthanded these days with the Persian war and the plague taking so many. But through it all, there are always affairs of state that need our attention.

ISHTAR: Life goes on, even during an apocalypse.

ISIS: Yes, I will stay a while. I do well with young ones.

MAL.: Then it's settled. Come! To the nursery!

(Lights change to nursery. All move to space with a burning fireplace, and a tall stout column that supports the roof. The child is in a crib. ISHTAR picks him up, as ISIS stops transfixed by the center post.)

ISHTAR: *(Holding the child)* Here's my little darling, what a sweet young pup.

MAL.: *(To ISIS)* Are you not well?

ISIS: I'm fine. The scent in this room. It reminds me of . . . happier times.

MAL.: Yes, that central column comes from a most rare fragrant tree; my woodsmen found it at the edge of the woods, growing alone with no like trees near.

ISIS: It is most rare, indeed.

ISHTAR: Then you should feel quite at home, this fire is cozy against the chill, and there's a pallet if you should drowse. *(She gives child to ISIS.)*

MAL.: The prince does like a lullaby, ever so often, if he gets cross . . .

ISHTAR: . . . Not that he will.

ISIS: Look how he sucks my fingertips.

ISHTAR: Whatever else you may need, just yell for a servant and it's yours. We are quite late for a reception with the Hittite ambassador; come my dear.
(They exit. ISIS places child back in crib and goes to post. Music.)
ISIS: Is it really you, my king? Is my long search to end at last? Are you somehow a prisoner of this tree, waiting for my love to break you free? *(Column pulsates and glows.)* Am I driven to delusion by longing? Do I imagine you to be so near? *(Column throbs.)* Oh my lord, the scent of your power overwhelms my womanly composure! *(She falls prostrate at his feet.)* Osiris! Great King and God! How could I have doubted the very son of Ra? Don't you know me, my king? It is your Isis. She who has ruled beside you since the beginning. What have I done? I have done everything. When you went traveling through the world teaching husbandry and music, though you were gone for a thousand seasons, I have protected your sovereignty. I have done everything. I have ruled Nubia in truth and dignity when you were gone all those years. And when you died, did I not mourn? I cut down a lock of my hair in mourning. My cries of grief, echoing off the far mountains, disturbed the sleep of our ancestors. I have done everything! Have looked for you down the sacred river and when the river ran into the great green sea, I became a sailor searching faithfully knowing you were somewhere waiting for the warmth of my breast to burn away the ice of death! *(The child cries.)* Hush little prince, do not be frightened. Only sounds of joy must fill this happy day. Smile for me, little one, for you have brought me to my husband's side. You have greatly pleased two Immortal Gods and for that your reward should be equally great. I know! I shall make you Immortal. Your mamma and papa will be so pleased when they discover that you will live eternally. Now don't be scared, little prince, for I must first burn your mortality away in the fire. You will feel no pain I promise you; I have done this millions of times and have yet to hurt anyone. Here we go . . .
(She holds him in the fireplace. ISHTAR enters.)
ISHTAR: By the Gods! NO!! *(She takes child from ISIS, pushing her aside.)*
ISIS: He was in no real danger! *(MAL. enters.)*
ISHTAR: She was holding him in the fire! A common child murderess!!
MAL.: Is that any way to repay our hospitality?

ISIS: You don't understand. I was in the process of making him immortal. I can do such things, you see, because I am a goddess.

ISHTAR: A goddess? I knew there was something strange about you.

ISIS: I am Isis, Queen of the Morning Star and holder of dozens of titles. My supernatural instincts tell me that somewhere in that post yonder is my dead king and husband Osiris, of whom I have already spoken. Nothing would please me more than to be able to take him back home.

MAL.: Axe-man! We will get to the heart of this mystery, and if all is as you say, you may take him home at once, with our blessing. (AXE-MAN *enters with axe.*) Chop it open!

(With one blow, the post splits in two revealing the sarcophagus with OSIRIS' *face showing through.)*

ISIS: Osiris!

ISHTAR: It's true. You ARE gods! Welcome both to our humble palace!

MAL.: Did you really make our son immortal?

ISIS: That chance is gone forever; interruption broke the spell. But, sucking from the goddess's fingers assures him of a long and happy life.

ISHTAR: We are most grateful.

MAL.: Go with our humble blessing. My men will see you to the riverbank, from there, you must hire a boat. Your journey will likely be a bitter one.

ISIS: I am not worried. Osiris will be my captain.

(Attendants lift sarcophagus as ISIS *bows farewell to her hosts, they leave in procession with* ISIS *following,* ISHTAR *and* MAL. *wave to her as lights go to out.)*

Scene 4

(SETH sits on the throne. He is attended by courtier and servants who feed him fruit, and fan him with palm leaves, etc. Enter a NOBLEMAN.)

NOBLE: My lord, the people cry out in hunger and strife as they watch their crops shrivel like the bellies of their livestock! The ribs of many can be counted at fifty paces. There is serious unrest in the provinces, as rebel leaders stir the people against you. You must raise a great army to contain the coming uprising or the kingdom will be lost to the scorpions!

SETH: Be gone from me, messenger of despair. (SETH *kills the NOBLE with a spear. He's pulled away by a guard.*) What care I of these troubles? Let my people feed on each other in a cannibalistic frenzy. I sense a far greater challenge to my power, with the return of my once-dead brother. He comes this way as surely as the dawn, accompanied by his traitorous wife. There is a mighty battle coming, and at its end, in victory I will send him into oblivion. I will fight him arrow for arrow, matching him in fierceness. Blood from our battle will fertilize the fields of Nubia. I will use compassion like a painted harlot and charity like a whipping-boy. I will forge in victory such a power as the world has never known! Will massage the lizard brain of entire populations! Holocausts! Fireworks! Electrocutions by manufactured lightning! Let the saints march in to save him; I will march them out again!

Scene 5
(The sarcophagus floats down the Nile on a small barge with a triangular sail. Music. ISIS sits sidesaddle on the breast of OSIRIS' casket. The blue-green waves of the river billow around them. ISIS hums a sad pretty melody as she tenderly strokes the carved brow.)
ISIS: *(She hums her tune.)* I sing my contentment to our mother the sky-woman arching her starry body over all. *(She hums.)* Satisfaction and eager longing jostle each other for room in my crowded heart. To have my Lord so near and all but present with touching, smells; O sandalwood skin drowning the air with male perfume! And yet. And yet, to know I bear you home to an unsure life, that may more resemble living death. Seth, our brother, plots to chop you up and feed you to the crocodiles, so relentless is his jealous fury. But I cannot dwell on violence in a night so rich in splendor! *(She hums her tune, and removes the lid of the sarcophagus.)* A night which blesses our holy reunion. *(She places herself on top of his body.)* I will stretch full length upon you, my divine divan; my celestial chaise lounge. Ah! Who could resist such comfort! Snug and secure as a cradle. Oh yes. I shall sleep this night in a deep land, that I have not visited for long long years!
(Sings)
What's this feeling in my heart?
I can't name it, yet it's so familiar
Just when understanding starts

I lose it, and it slips away—
But it must be love, the love I have for you;
I remember like it was just this morning,
When I held you in my arms, and
We would always remember to say, (I want you to know)
It's only you inside my heart,
Can't quite name it, yet it's so familiar;
I'll never let you get away from me again!
No, not to stay! As long as I have you,
There's nothing I can't do!
I can't let you get away. I need you everyday!
I can't let you get away. I need you. I need you. I need you. I
need you night and day . . .
(Waves billow wildly as OSIRIS' *arms reach up to encircle* ISIS.*)*
Oh captain! Steer thy vessel into my wild harbor! Oh! Oh!! Aim
thy prow into the silt of my fertile delta! Oh!
*(They become hidden by the waves for a moment. Waves and
music build to a climax. Lights change as waves subside revealing*
ISIS *and* OSIRIS *thrown separately onto the riverbank.* ISIS *rouses
herself and gives birth to* HORUS. *He is a full-grown hawk-headed
golden warrior.)*
ISIS: With our son beside us, born of impossible love, we will
challenge evil and send it howling to the nether regions!

Scene 6
*(*SETH's *kingdom. Red with gloom. Two citizens speak furtively on
the streets of the capital.)*
MAN: Is it true? I hear our days of misery dwindle to an end. I'm
afraid to believe it.
WOMAN: Yes. By the wings of Thoth, I swear it. Osiris, though he
be dead, lives again! He comes home with beloved Isis to free
heaven and earth from bondage and blood. And with him, O
wondrous miracle! He brings a son, fierce and sure-sighted as
the hawk, born of the goddess in the tall papyrus where the
mouth of the Nile kisses the sea!
MAN: I've almost forgotten the sound of my own children's laughter.
How I long for that sweet noise to again fill my gloomy rooms.
Fear and dread too often fill our calendar. Seth the Pitiless
rewards only cruelty, and makes compassion into sin.
WOMAN: In truth, a generation falls deep into his spell and grows
forgetful of the time when Great Osiris ruled in harmony . . .

MAN: But evil and strife shall lift like dewy fog dispelled by morning sun, when Isis and Osiris return.

WOMAN: May Hathor hasten the day!

MAN: Quiet now! Here come Seth and his cabinet . . . (MAN and WOMAN exit as SETH and HAPSUT, a general, enter.)

SETH: Does my brother dream that I will let him near my city, to again work his spell? Whether he is dead, or sleeping dreaming death, he holds the power to create new gods to take his side against me. But my determination to rule is as hearty as my lust for his sweet wife. I would sever my own head, before harming a hair on hers . . .

HAPSUT: Here, my lord, lives the wizard whose powers I know well. Ho! Wizard! Rouse yourself and bow before great Seth, the Master of Creation!

WIZARD: What odorous spit-frog wakes me from my nap? This better be good . . .

HAPSUT: It is none other than the mighty king of night, Great Seth! Bow down, wild turkey!

WIZARD: Hail, masters. I would really love to bow this ancient body down before your eminences, but the years have turned my bending-joints to stone. Therefore, accept my sincere hail, even though I offer it from an upstanding position.

SETH: Are you the sorcerer who conjures great monstrosities?

WIZARD: In my time, a time or two were as you have heard.

SETH: Let me join my magic with yours, and we will fashion an indestructible demon, for he must be strong enough to challenge the resurrected god. To your dark incantations, add my accomplishments for yeast. Take disillusionment, lost hope, diseases of the mind and of the soul, false truths! Sworn lies of tribes and nations! Supernatural corruption . . .

WIZARD: Hold on! Give me time to prepare the proper, eh, preparations! I don't want to miss this opportunity to go beyond the limits of ordinary evil. (WIZARD puts on crown, cape, and staff; he chants a magic spell.) Azzara Rhosta Magnah Bhostu! Azzara Rhosta Magnah Bhostum! Abzzada Xszo! Xzso Tintullum! (To SETH) Give me your worse now, master, and we'll put it in the brew!

SETH: Come, crimes against creation! Perversion of the Law! Deliberate ignorance! Virulent confusion . . .!

WIZARD: Enough! Stop it, or I'll not be responsible for the mischief you unleash!

SETH: Meaningless War! Come look upon your master!
WIZARD: By the warts of the sacred vulture, here he comes!!!
(A gigantic white dragon-headed snake appears. It breathes smoke from nostrils and gills, dances menacingly, then coils itself loosely around SETH.)
SETH: Go forth, Great Sorrow-Maker! Seek my brother Osiris and devour him! Deliver havoc to his unsuspecting corpse, rendering it beyond salvation! But bring me Isis as a souvenir. Now, GO!
(Snake exits as lights fade to out.)

Scene 7
(ISIS and HORUS have paused on the journey home. They rest on OSIRIS' casket. ISIS massages her foot.)
ISIS: We are very near home, by the way the wind blows north. I'll be ready to lie in my own bedchamber for a change.
HORUS: I need. Something.
ISIS: What, precious one?
HORUS: To know. Myself.
ISIS: That's easy! You are Horus, my son, whose coming was foretold. You are born of Isis and Osiris. Do you know them?
HORUS: What creature does not.
ISIS: You were born to unify the world; to bring harmony back to fashion.
HORUS: What is Har Mon Nee?
ISIS: Harmony is the beginning of truth. Without it, chaos reigns.
HORUS: The world has become filled with new-style devils since I was last here.
ISIS: You begin to remember yourself. Soon you will remember all.
HORUS: I must avenge my royal father.
ISIS: Osiris, do you hear? He's a little one-man army . . .!
HORUS: I must avenge Nubia!
ISIS: All in good time, my little falcon. First come suckle. You must grow strong for the battles ahead. *(HORUS sits on her lap and feeds from ISIS' breast. Drums begin. A loud animal roar sounds off stage)* What is that? Thunder from a clear sky?
BEAST: *(In a distorted monster voice)* It is I, unlucky warriors; the Bottomless Devourer of Universes! The Mindless Terror! *(The BEAST enters, breathing smoke.)*
ISIS: It is our destiny to battle you, heinous one! See how his very breath pollutes the air!

BEAST: Beware, brave warriors, who would come near my jaws. I will eat your valor in a flash, and leave a pile of smoking bones!

ISIS : Take the sword from your father's still hand and defend us!

BEAST: Be warned, you foolish masters, who would raise a sword against me! My wounds drip a poisoned blood that dissolves eternity. My fiery breath will burn creation like a pile of straw!

(HORUS *stands before him with raised sword.*)

Your childish courage is a threadbare blanket against the chill of ten million winters living in my determination! Prepare to die and be forgotten! (*Surrounds them with his body, raises his head to strike.*)

HORUS: By the power of resurrection and rebirth, I say NO! (*He strikes* BEAST *who then breaks into many pieces, the pieces scurry away howling to exit.*) What smoky hell could cough up such a mighty worm?

ISIS: Not hell, but the mind of your Uncle Seth. I think that thing was our welcoming committee from the false king.

HORUS: My uncle? I can't wait to show him gratitude.

(HORUS *wipes the sword and places it in his belt, as lights fade to out.*)

Scene 8

(SETH *sits on the throne.* HAPSUT *sits at his feet.*)

SETH: Will I ever love again? Really love, like when I was a hard red boy hunting foxes in the summer grass?

HAPSUT: But lord; do not forget your lovely wife Nephthys. Her beauty is as renowned as her sister, Isis.

SETH: But they are as alike as night and morning. Isis is the rising sun. Her sister is the Empress of the Age of Ice.

HAPSUT: Did she not bear your excellent son Anubis?

SETH: That dog is not my son! It just isn't possible. Never could I penetrate the Arctic Circle. Anubis is my brother's bastard freak.

HAPSUT: Osiris?

SETH: None other. One more monstrous insult my brother planned with great precision.

HAPSUT: He is, after all, the god of perfection, you know.

SETH: Watch it. You risk execution by pointing out an obvious truth to a superior.

(ATTENDANT *hands a scroll to* HAPSUT. *He reads it.*)

HAPSUT: I fear I must do even worse. This dispatch from the watchtower tells of three weary gods coming towards the city. One woman, one dead man, and one who flies like a hawk.

SETH: Curse creation! They're supposed to be destroyed! Your wizard is a lizard! You have misled me! *(He kills* HAPSUT.*)* Such wonderful wickedness wasted forever . . .

(ISIS, HORUS *and* OSIRIS *enter.)*

ISIS: Evil spent makes way for good.

SETH: Isis, my sister! Back so soon? And I see you've brought the big stiff with you! But who is this Birdman?

HORUS: Seize him for the murder of my father Osiris! Put him in chains!

SETH: Your father? Very interesting, prince, eh . . .?

ISIS: He is called Horus, the guardian eagle.

SETH: Horus, my dear nephew, your very existence proves that Osiris is not dead! The dead, despite their great numbers, do not breed.

HORUS: You are as slippery as the water snake.

SETH: But, far more charming, wouldn't you agree, Isis? Or have you grown so accustomed to the living dead, that you forget the inner heat of flesh.

HORUS: Exile him! Send the usurper to wander the wastelands!

SETH: I ruled as best I could in your absence! It wasn't easy, either, considering the state Osiris left things in. There was a lot of housecleaning to do thanks to his liberal policies!

*(*HORUS *lunges toward* SETH*; he is restrained by* ISIS.*)*

ISIS: Wait, my son. Let us chasten our emotions and think to the good of our great kingdom. Seth has done wicked things, but our nation needs him. His warmth alone bursts the seed at planting time, and dries the valley after the life-giving flood.

HORUS: But mother he . . .

ISIS: With you here now, to guard against his excesses, we must use his benefits, and keep his harm in check. In this way we will once again restore harmony to our wounded land.

1ST PRIESTESS: And the people let out a clamor of relief, shouting their praise for the restored order of the world! Praise for Isis!

ALL: Isis! Isis!

2ND For Osiris! For Horus, the mighty hawk!

3RD And for Seth, he who completes the Holy reunion!

ALL: May they ride upon the boat of one million years!

(All four take position on the throne, which is not big enough; all jostle for position as lights fade.

END OF ACT ONE

ACT TWO
Scene I
(A tranquil domestic scene at court. ISIS sits having her hair dressed by two attendants. Another attendant tends to OSIRIS' beard. A harpist plays softly. ANUBIS, the dogheaded son of NEPHTHYS, plays a game rolling a ball with a stick. PRIESTESS lights an offering at a small altar. All is lit by shafts of afternoon sunlight.)

1ST PRIESTESS: *(Coming forward.)* The world, for a time, basked in the reflected glow of a second golden age! For Great Osiris radiated honor, charity, and wisdom like a beacon, even in the half-life state which still possessed him. Great Isis, she who gives grace to strength, ruled beside him, mindful of his limitations, but content to guide his holy business, as well as tend to her own great mandate, while the snores of Osiris' eternal sleep, fell upon her ears as sweet as the songs of angels . . .

(ANUBIS drops the game and runs toward ISIS.)

ANUBIS: Tell me the story again, Aunt Isis . . .

ISIS: Which one, my little darling?

ANUBIS: You know; about the Queen of Syria, and the baby in the fireplace . . . and . . .!

ISIS: And your uncle imprisoned in the Tree of Life?

ANUBIS: Yes! That part's my favorite!

ISIS: *(Waves away attendants, who exit.)* First tell me of my sister, Nephthys. Is she well and good?

ANUBIS: My mother is the same, I guess. She takes to bed most days at dawn, with a great show of sighs, then sleeps in her darkened chamber till the moon has risen high above the highest watchtower. She thus avoids the doings of the day.

ISIS: . . . And the help of anyone who COULD help.

ANUB.: My mother hates me.

ISIS: Anubis! No mother can hate her child, even if he should die by her hand.

ANUB.: I don't mind it much. I'm used to it. My father is away, always fighting demons worse than himself. He is very brave and strong. But even he cannot look me in my eyes for more than a blink, before looking at his sandals.

ISIS: My arms are always open to you.

ANUB.: I know. See how Uncle Osiris' gaze never wavers from mine! And he smiles on me, without moving his lips. No matter where I run, his eyes follow me, clothing my soul in safety!

ISIS: That's his love you feel upon you.

ANUB.: I wish you were my parents. Why would the Goddess play such a trick?

ISIS: It is folly to question the wisdom of Hathor; it is as infinite as the sands.

ANUB.: It is?

ISIS: Come to me little one; sit on my lap like when you were a baby.

HORUS: *(Rushing on.)* Mother, kiss calm goodbye, for here returns my Uncle Seth fresh from his latest crusade. He is even fuller of himself than I thought possible, given the limitations of arrogance.

(Fanfare. A party of heralds enter with drums beating.)

HERALD: Great Isis, Queen of All Worlds! Mighty Osiris, Ruler of the dead, and of the living! Your noble Brother Seth returns with his fearless legions in triumph from the outer wars! Hail Great Seth!

(SETH enters amid shouts of Seth! Seth! Seth! etc. In one hand he is clutching the hair on the severed head of a large blue devil.)

SETH: Hail, my Sister Queen and Brother God! I award you the head of this demon king as a sign of my willingness to keep the nation free of upstart terrorists!

ISIS: Nubia welcomes her victorious Son.

CHORUS: Seth! Seth! Seth! Seth!!

ANUBIS: Hello F-Father . . .

SETH: Anubis? Is it you? How you have grown.

ISIS: Go to your, father, dear.

(ANUBIS stumbles as he crosses to SETH.)

SETH: Yes, you have grown clumsier and more stupid!

(Soldiers laugh; ANUBIS runs off in tears.)

ISIS: I see that cruelty is still wedded to your courage.

SETH: *(Spits)* He is an abomination! You should never have saved him from the burning desert! Nephthys was right to abandon him there. One of the few right things she's ever done.

ISIS: You and my unfortunate sister seem to forget that he is born of a god, as were we all. The two of you sometimes behave like the worst of mortals.

SETH: Look at the two of you! So smug in your superiority! Not everyone is fooled by your deceitfulness.

ISIS: Watch your tongue, or I will summon Horus to silence it!

SETH: *(Laughs softly)* No, dear Isis, not even you may spoil my homecoming. My men gave me brave support, and I'll not cheat them of the victory celebration they have earned by bloody service. Listen well to the wild cheers of the multitudes as we march among them. They have too long been without an active leader . . . *(He exits amid cries of Seth! Seth! Seth! All follow except ISIS and HORUS.)*

ISIS: This could be big trouble, my son.

HORUS: Let him not provoke me, for I will shatter his illusion of invincibility, should he again threaten the good order of the world.

ISIS: We must hide Osiris away from his brother's sight, for between his every word, I hear his madness driving him to destroy us.

HORUS: I have seen a secret cave, beyond the valley of the skulls, whose mouth is hidden by an ever-blooming bush. There we can secure him till Seth's craziness has cooled.

ISIS: *(She claps her hands to summon some attendants.)* That will do us well. Precaution is the mother of survival.

(All leave in procession carrying OSIRIS off in his sarcophagus. Lights down.)

Scene 2

(Two SOLDIERS stand outside the door to SETH's bedchamber; from within, SETH screams a long tortured howl; SOLDIERS bend in to listen.)

1ST SOLD.: Of late, he is too often thus; crying like the damned in hell.

(SETH screams again, more pitifully than before.)

2ND SOLD.: I hear a note in this howling like none before, in my time.

1ST.: You are green in these matters, I am a veteran of a thousand campaigns, and have only heard these sounds when he is near his family.

(SETH screams.)

1ST: He laments estrangement from his very kin. It is like the longing of the left hand for the touch of the severed right one. *(Noise within.)* What's that now? He comes this way, I'll not chance meeting him in such a mood! *(SOLD. starts out.)*

2ND.: I'm with you, brother! *(They exit.)*

SETH: *(Enters drunk and unkempt.)* Soldiers! Soldiers! Come back here so I can chop off your heads! Come to me when

I call, damned of the gods! Gone. All gone away. The wife I cannot bear to touch. Gone. The son who is not a son. Gone. Gone. Dear sister who despises me; dear brother who would sooner die than say my name aloud! Gone, gone, gone, gone, gone, gone; all gone forever! O Great Osiris! My brother! Everybody LOVES Osiris! Everybody thinks he's SOOO great. But what do you know! Only I can know what is in his heart of hearts. We are as twins who have held each other in the incomprehensible intimacy of the primordial waters. Even in death, he outshines me. Compared to his serenity, my conquests are as inconsequential nothings, forgotten overnight. His heart is cold with ambition. Be not fooled by his calm. His feet seek to rest on my windpipe. But I will enact a page from my manuscript of revenges! Yes! He who tries to conquer me, his son, my concubine will surely be . . .

Scene 3
(ISIS and HORUS at the palace. They are dressed in formal evening clothes. A meal is concluding.)

ISIS: You are of the same flesh and spirit as your Uncle Seth, it is true; your zeal is tempered by your love of justice, but we cannot deny you have some things in common with him.

HORUS: Seth is a tenacious hunter. Warriors have much in common with their enemies. But this is not love.

ISIS: I, for one, would rejoice if Seth would be our enemy no more. Go to him, Horus. But be careful. I'm happy he wants to see you. If the father's love he feels for you could tame his vengeful heart, what a world we would have then!

HORUS: He does put on a frightful show; but his courage and strong beliefs have earned him many admirers . . .

ISIS: Go to him, tonight, as he requests. Go with our blessing, if you decide to do so.

HORUS: I'll go to him. This very night as he requests. But I'll not let my guard down for a moment.

ISIS: As long as you make the effort . . .

HORUS: His charming tongue has wrought many cunning seductions. But I will measure every word.

ISIS: Good. Don't let his tongue near your person.

HORUS: Don't worry! If he wishes to form a new alliance, I am willing to discuss it, but there are certain conditions that must first be met.

ISIS: What conditions?

HORUS: Firstly, he must never again try to destroy Father.

ISIS: That's good. What else?

HORUS: He should cease and desist his foolish attempts to get you into his bed.

ISIS: Good luck with that one. Is there another?

HORUS: And most important, he must never, by thought or action, by magic or luck, set out to deliberately upset the ancient balance of power.

ISIS: That he'll never agree to. But all you can do is try.

HORUS: Do not forget, mother, that I am not without my own powers of persuasion.

ISIS: I suspect you may need them and more. Go, may the gods protect you. *(Lights down.)*

Scene 4
(SETH's bedchamber. SETH stands c. as HORUS enters and pauses at the doorway.)

SETH: Don't be afraid, nephew. Come in. I've been expecting you.

HORUS: In your private chamber?

SETH: You're as timid as a virgin. It's all right. We're both gods, aren't we?

(HORUS comes in, and begins looking around the room.)

SETH: Do you like music?

HORUS: Of course; my father invented it you know.

SETH: Oh yes, one of his many accomplishments. *(Claps hands and music begins. Nat King Cole sings "Nature Boy." HORUS picks up an ornate bow from SETH's collection.)* Do you like it?

HORUS: An excellent bow. *(He strikes an archer's pose. SETH comes behind him and places his hands upon HORUS')*

SETH: It is a present from Bes, a strange little god I met on my travels through the southern Sudan. *(HORUS slips from his embrace.)*

HORUS: Why have you sent for me?

SETH: Is it not obvious? I'm weary of the constant bickering between our camps. What a monumental waste of time war is. You and I have much in common, after all.

HORUS: Like what?

SETH: We both love your mother, for one thing. What a great woman! No kingdom could ask for a finer goddess . . .

HORUS: Why now, after so much treachery?

SETH: Times have changed. I wish to have peace in my own family, and you are the key. Will you drink a friendship cup with me? (ATTENDANT *brings tray with pitcher and two cups.* SETH *hands one to* HORUS *and takes one himself.*) Let's forget about the quarrels of the past. *(They drink.* HORUS *makes a face.)* I was young and impulsive with a nasty temper, much like your own, I'll bet. How is your drink?

HORUS: Strong! But good. *(Drains cup.)* More!

SETH: *(Pours drink)* Careful young stallion, else you'll be kicking like a mule.

HORUS: *(Drinks)* I feel . . . dizzy. *(He stands unsteadily.)*

SETH: This way, nephew; to my bed. *(SETH rises and leads him to lie down.)*

HORUS: The room spins and spins like a whirlpool! I can't make it stop!

SETH: Fear not, little Horus; I know a sure way to stop it.

HORUS: *(Lying down.)* I feel like I'm falling into a dream . . .

SETH: Yes, I feel it too. Let me douse this lamplight. *(He signals and lights dim.)* Now come closer, little lamb of gold, and we will dream in tandem . . . *(Lights out)*

Scene 5

(ISIS paces back and forth. Downstage, the PRIESTESS addresses us.)

PRIESTESS: In despair Isis walked the palace colonnade, sure her advice had sent sweet Horus to an early doom. It was breaking dawn before the sound of her son's footsteps released her heartbeat from the grip of dread . . . *(PRIEST. exits.)*

ISIS: I was sick with worry. Did you lose track of time?

HORUS: I fell asleep. My uncle drugged me with a powerful liquor which turned all sensations into blissful dream.

ISIS: What sort of dream?

HORUS: Most strange and sweet. I dreamed of a great stone knife, churning between my legs for butter. When I woke, I was alone, and in my hand, I held these seeds.

ISIS: Oh Horus! Seth has mounted you like a she-camel in her sleep, and you have caught his seed in your hand! Quickly! We must chop it off, at once, or he will forever have authority over you. *(She chops it off with a sword.)*

HORUS: Mother! My hand! *(He shows stump.)*

ISIS: Fortunately for you, I am goddess of magic and medicine. I can make a new hand grow for you, by blowing on your stump . . . (*She blows and new hand appears.*)

HORUS: Nice work, this. (*He looks at new hand.*)

ISIS: That was close. Shame on Seth for taking advantage of your green nature. So he wishes to play that game, does he? I know a way that we may turn his little joke back upon him. Your uncle's weakness for the honeydew melon is well known.

HORUS: True. He would sooner feast on honeydew, than on a roasted oryx heart.

ISIS: We will prepare a fruit of irresistible delicacy (*She holds melon*) made potent by a contribution from your sacred loins. Take your knife and cut a plug from its side, like this; take it into your room and . . . (*She whispers to him.*)

HORUS: But Mother, I . . . Oh! I see! I will plow it well for planting! (*Takes melon and exits.*)

ISIS: That's the way, my son. Good night; or shall I say, good morning . . .! (*Lights out.*)

Scene 6

(SETH *at a table eating.* 1ST SOLDIER *brings him the melon on a dish, and* SETH *begins to eat it.*)

SETH: Um! This honeydew has a sweetness to it like youth itself. Ah! Such intangible satisfaction from such a simple fruit. I feel it nourishing my very soul with its exceptional juices. (*He greedily stuffs it into his mouth.* 2ND SOLDIER *enters.*)

2ND SOLDIER: Hail Master! I report good news! Our hunters have located the hiding-place of your brother's body.

SETH: Good! Where?!

2ND SOLD.: In a small cave beyond the Valley of The Skulls.

HORUS: Who guards him?

SOLD.: None, my lord. Only a bush which hides the entrance.

HORUS: Let us attend to him at once! Now I will come into my own, as was long ago foretold. I will cause him such mutilations that our mother Nut will not recognize her firstborn twin! Bring me my sword! I will dismember him limb from limb and joint from joint, scattering the pieces to the open jaws of the crocodile! Vengeance!! (*Exit, amid cries of* Seth! Seth! Seth! etc.)

Scene 7

(ISIS *and a young girl who sits weaving at a loom.*)

ISIS: Push harder on that treadle, if you wish to make your pattern sing.

GIRL: My legs cramp, madam. And my fingers grow stiff.

ISIS: Then rest a while. You have worked hard . . . (*Sound of chopping off*) What was that noise?

GIRL: I hear nothing.

ISIS: I, too, am tired today, perhaps tomorrow we will . . . (*Chopping sound.*) Do you not hear that? A sound like a woodsman felling a far off tree? (*Dog barks.*)

GIRL: I hear only the barking of a dog.

ISIS: That's my nephew, Anubis. He's my little protector while my Osiris is . . . (*She starts, as if struck by vision.*) OSIRIS!!!

(*Lights down*)

Scene 8

(SETH *in shadow, raises a great axe and chops down in rhythm.*)

SETH: O, my accursed brother! (*Chop.*) I loathe you with an aching passion. (*Chop.*) Your perfume is a stench in my nostrils more foul than the rotten breath of vultures! (*Chop.*) Your silent virtue curses my ears with accusations! (*Chop.*) Your smug security leaves a silver slug trail across my spirit! (*Chop.*) I hate you with a healing force! (*Chop.*) Your notoriety longs to penetrate my obscurity! (*Chop!*) But that will never be! (*Chop.*) I will reduce you to useless parts, fit only for digestion by the beasts of the Nile! (*Chop, chop, chop!*) I will transform your glory into crocodile shit!

SOLD.: What should we do with these pieces, Master?

SETH: Throw them into the river, you idiot! Haven't you been listening? Let the tide serve him up for supper! (*Wail of mourning begins soft at first, but building to include all voices. It dies away, until it again becomes a single voice.*) (*Lights go to dawn*)

Scene 9

(*Lights go to dawn as* PRIESTESS *walks through the Nile waters. Three* WOMEN *are near her washing clothes.*)

PRIESTESS: The following dawn three women of the city washed their garments in the sacred Nile. As they washed, they sang a song even older than laundry.

1ST WM.: *(Sings)* Where was my husband last night? Why does he always have to get into a fight?

2ND WM.: To prove he's a man to some other man . . .

ALL: Somehow, it doesn't seem right.

3RD WM.: Where was your husband, ask you? Out with a buddy or two.

1ST WM.: Blood stains and wine stains from belly to chin . . .

2ND WM.: He comes home, finds the key; but he can't put it in . . .

3RD: So he's able to sleep in the stable all night.

ALL: Somehow, it doesn't seem right!

1ST WM: *(Spoken)* I know I've said it before, girls, but this time I mean it. If that low life so and so hits me one more time, I'm leaving him for good! Even if it means living in the streets.

2ND: And what of your children?

1ST: Let them fend for themselves for a while. They're all walking. What do I care what people say about it. Everyone knows I'm common as dirt.

3RD: Common as CLAY, dear. It's not quite so harsh.

2ND: I wish my husband were still alive. I wouldn't care if he did hit me. He didn't have much of a punch anyway. Not nearly as hard to bear as this sickening emptiness that I jokingly refer to as my life.

1ST: Careful, don't be so irreverent. The river has ears, and she remembers all.

3RD: That's right. Ears and other senses befitting a great immortal.

2ND: Oh! I thought it was the little minnows trying to nibble my pubis. *(Laughs)*

1ST: Silence! Do you not sense the presence of the Ancient and Good?

3RD: I smell sandalwood.

2ND: . . . One whose song brought forth the world?

1ST: You are right, sisters. I am a priestess of Osiris. Only his divine body mixing with the waters could cause this eerie color.

2ND: Something is wrong. Something terrible . . .

1ST: Feel how the very pressure drops to the bottom!

3RD: *(Screams)* Look! Look! *(She picks up chunk of a leg.)* Is it not my lord's holy shank? And look, here float more pieces. Great Osiris has been rent asunder like a beef at market. Look how these sacred steaks roll upon the waters like the discarded cargo of a slaughterhouse!!

1ST: Sister, control your hysterical ravings, and help the cause. These are indeed the piteous remains of Great Osiris. See. They have been untouched by scavengers. We must gather them all and return them to great Isis. She will know what to do with them.

Scene 10

(ISIS *and* HORUS *at palace. Attendants rush about a scene of disarray. There is a great moaning and wailing in grief.*)

ISIS: Don't blame yourself, Horus. All is not lost.

HORUS: I should have guarded him. But where was I? Circling high in the sky hunting small prey . . .

ISIS: Nothing can change what has come to pass. At least his head is whole. Be thankful that we have gathered up so many pieces of him from the Nile.

HORUS: Thank the King of the Crocodiles for that. He forbade his people to eat even a bite of Father as he floated temptingly by their mouths.

ISIS: It won't be easy putting these pieces back together again. It was lucky you were able to recover so much, except . . . wait; where is his phallus?!

HORUS: I'm afraid the little crabs heeded not the words of the Crocodile King. They made a meal of his manroot.

ISIS : So be it. I will have to fashion him another. I know. I will take one of my ribs and work it into the proper shape. (*She turns her back and reaches into her robe and pulls out a curved bone.*) That will serve us both well. (*She places bone.*)

HORUS: I must be after Seth, before he gets too far away! Osiris LIVES! (*He exits.*)

(*River* WOMEN *enter carrying bundled pieces of* OSIRIS.)

ISIS: And what do you three sisters bring? Tribute from the river?

1ST: Great Lady, we bring a most sacred offering plucked from the breast of the mother Nile. Osiris' rendered meat we found downstream while doing our laundry.

ISIS: The fragrance alone tells me that these are some of the missing parts of the god. You have done well, sisters of the Nile.

2ND: We knew you would know what to do, great goddess.

ISIS: The first thing I must do is reward you for your steadfastness and quick action. You three are hereby designated Priestesses of Isis, and are eligible for all honors and entitlements due your sacred status.

2ND: Gee! I don't know what to say!

3RD: Does that mean we get new outfits?

1ST: I'm already a priestess of Osiris.

ISIS: These are simple matters for the Goddess of Morn. (*Claps her hands and attendants help three women change to regal robes.*)
ALL: Thanks! Thank you! How wonderful! Etc.
ISIS: And now for the hard work. Let's put him back together. I'll need all our power to make a picture of this puzzle!
NEPHYTHS (*enters*): Am I too late? Don't start without me . . .
ISIS: Royal Nephthys! My sister; your skill is required too, if this nation is ever to be whole again. Come with me now; give me your subtle assistance if we ever want to see Osiris walking!
(*Women work on body, binding it with mummy cloth. Nephthys turns and faces audience.*)
NEPHT.: Yeah, I'm Nephthys, the twin sister of princess Goody-Two-Shoes over there. I know, you think I'm selfish, a bad mother, and I chain smoke too if you must know. Judge me if you must, but you will never understand my feelings. You, with your mortal imagination, will never comprehend what's happening to my nervous system. All my feelings, no matter how petty they may seem to you, are happening to me in cosmic proportions. Try to visualize infinite pain. You can't, can you? But I came, in spite of all my burdens, to do what I can to help in this time of need. For amid the debris of years of humiliating disappointments, one god went out of his way to get me pregnant, even though he knew it was certain to cause a scandal. Only he was powerful enough to take that risk in order that I could have something I needed for me. Is that so wrong?
ANUBIS: Hello, M-mother.
NEPHT.: My little one. Come hug your mother. (*They hug.*) Ouch. You are brittle from neglect.
ANUBIS: I'm sorry.
NEPTH.: No. It is I who am the sorry one.
ISIS: Nephthys! Come, we need all hands on this job!
NEPTH.: Let's go, Anubis! We must put your father back together now!
ISIS: It is about time! Join us in a prayer to our great mother Hathor. O sublime Hathor!
ALL: O Sublime Hathor!
ISIS: Mother of Universes! We call upon your healing power to aid us in this great task!
ALL: Help us Mother of Universes!
ISIS: Help us bind the wounds that separate your son Osiris from himself.

ALL: Guide our hands, Great One.

NEPTH.: Not that we dare question your great wisdom, great mother, that allowed him to be chopped up like this in the first place. But since you did so, Holy Hathor, it is the least you can do to lend us your sacred fluids to glue him back together, restoring the beautiful form he had in life.

1ST: Come, Luminous One. Restore his broken flesh with your sweet breath!

ISIS: O Venerable Mother . . .

ALL: You-Who-Would-Make-Right-Use-Of-The-Heart . . .

ISIS: Help us reunite his members to their former wholeness. And restore his great soul to the seat of Atum-Ra!

ALL: And restore his great soul to the seat of Atum-Ra!!

ISIS: That's all we can do. Let's stand him up and unwrap him.

(Music. WOMEN *unwind strips of cloth from* OSIRIS *revealing him whole again. Cheers and shouts as* NEPHTHYS *places the flail in* OSIRIS' *right hand and* ISIS *places the crook in his left.* OSIRIS *sits stiffly on the throne flanked by the two goddesses. A fanfare sounds and* HORUS *enters.*)

HORUS: Look! My father, Great Osiris, is restored to us! How was this miracle done?

ISIS: Nephthys and I called upon our grandmother Hathor for an ounce of her healing power to put with our own. The result you see before you.

HORUS: Hail, Father of faith! Behold! (*Attendants bring in* SETH *crouching in a small cage.*) Here is the cursed assassin who has twice dared murder Nubia! Hang him high as a testament to the futility of evil. (*Cage is suspended on a hook and raised above the heads of the others.*) Forgive my youthful inattention, Father; it distracted me from my prime duty!

ISIS: You have done well, Horus.

HORUS: Take him, mother, and fashion what punishment you see fit for such a criminal. But try to divorce compassion from your revenge for a change. The remnants of Seth's army hide in the wilderness and plot to carry out their master's wishes to the death. I will seek them out, and not return till the last of their murderous mouths is filled with sand!

(HORUS *exits followed by all but* ISIS, OSIRIS, *and the caged* SETH. *A pause.* SETH *whimpers softly in the silence.*)

ISIS: Is your pain so great?

SETH: Yessssss! Your son nearly bit my arm clean through. And there was much undue kicking and scratching after I had already surrendered. He is a bully, and a cruel one. These wounds will never heal without your kiss upon them. *(Pause)* Won't you kiss my hurt? Please!? Osiris won't mind. See how well you have restored him! I never intended that he should be fragmented for all time . . . Together we have fulfilled his destiny. *(Offers bandaged arm through cage bars.)* Please. Won't you? *(Slowly, ISIS rises and tenderly kisses it.)* Ah! Thank you. Feels better already! *(He removes bandage.)* What do you intend to do with me now? Let me rot in this rat cage?

ISIS: I might. It would make a compelling display, for all who know the story.

SETH: My powers will grow weak if I crouch too long in this position.

ISIS: Good.

SETH: Isis, be reasonable, won't you? Compassion is the sweet fruit of enlightenment, and you are the goddess of both compassion and enlightenment. Would you go against your very nature? Let me out. It would honor our sacred mother . . .

ISIS: You dare to speak of honor.

SETH: My dear, divine sister, the people need my hot spark, you know. Sow the grain, but try and make it sprout without me. And whose heat but mine will dry out the land after the flood? Is that how Isis wants to be remembered, as the authoress of famine? Let me out. I'll be good. Good for Nubia. Good for the world. Did you not restore Osiris? I am powerless beside such a miracle. Please?

ISIS: May the gods forgive me. *(Cage is lowered to the floor, and ISIS unlocks it.)* You are my brother, and in truth, your suffering blends into my own. I cannot let you suffer in sight.

SETH: *(Gets out of cage and stretches his limbs.)* Thank you. That wasn't so bad now was it? I've worked up quite an appetite in solitary; is there any food and drink about?

(ISIS claps her hands and musicians and dancers bring in a banquet, and serve SETH who eats with lust and relish. Someone brings him a cut piece of honeydew melon.)

SETH: Ah! my favorite dish! You are too kind to remember it . . .!

ISIS: Seth, there is something I must tell you about that, you see . . .

(Music stops as HORUS flies in from above.)

HORUS: Mother no! You have released my father's killer! You both mock my piety and shall be punished for it.

ISIS: No, my son . . .!
(With a swift blow, HORUS *severs the head of* ISIS. *She falls and is assisted by* ANUBIS *who has come in during the banquet. He replaces her head with the head of* HATHOR.*)*
HORUS: Mother, what magic is this? Are you Hathor now?
ISIS/HATHOR: I have always been she.
HORUS: But, I don't understand . . . I don't . . .!
ISIS/HATHOR: It was ever a mystery.
SETH: Come here, my little catamite! Let me give those buns another roasting!
*(*SETH *and* HORUS *clash.)*
HORUS: Your unholy seed sprouted not, my impotent uncle, for I caught it in my palm. But you did for a fact suck down the fecund juice of honeydew fortified with my fertility!
SETH: You! What?? Noooo!
HORUS: It is true, pus of creation! Your swollen belly holds my healthy children. *(He lunges, and* SETH *trips him: when he is down,* SETH *plucks out* HORUS' *right eye, sending him into a rage of pain.)* Owwww! Give me back my eye, monster, or never again will the moon bring her snows to the far-off mountain!
SETH: Come on! Take it back, if you can!
ISIS: Enough of this! Come sisters! *(*ISIS, NEPHTHYS *and others restrain* SETH *as* HORUS *pries the glowing eye from* SETH's *fist.* HORUS *takes the eye and crosses to* OSIRIS. *With a gentle motion, he places it in* OSIRIS' *mouth. Osiris swallows, lights change as he begins to move his limbs. Osiris walks toward* SETH *who cowers in fear. With a single blow, he strikes* SETH *dead.* ALL *stare in wonder.)*
OSIRIS: I! AM! OSIRIS! Judge of hearts, source of souls, undertaker to the living, midwife to the dead. All the world resonates with my vibration. Through tribulation and redemption, through faith and passion, I have broken the great chain of death and resurrection! Now will I return to Maat and prepare a place for those who will come after me! *(A golden ladder appears, and* OSIRIS *begins to climb.)* Farewell, you perfect imperfections! I will be with you again in paradise. *(Assembly weeps as* OSIRIS *disappears into a cloud.)*
ISIS: Do not weep! Let us all rejoice we gods and mortals, for Osiris' reconstruction. All our soul's salvation lies assured! Just as his great body and great soul are joined as one forever, so may we

too climb to paradise with all sins forgiven, and spirits as light as the feather in his crown!

HORUS: And like the mother Nile flows eternally changing, eternally unchanged so flows his blood through our hearts! Farewell father! I will rule the world forever mindful of your tenderness!

ALL: Farewell, sweet father, farewell . . .! (*Drummers and dancers break into a song of great celebration as* OSIRIS *disappears from view.*)

2ND PRIESTESS: And when Great Osiris had returned to the grounded waters of being, Isis and Horus sat together on the throne and presided over the Third Golden Age of Harmony that lasted until the age of the Pharaohs.

(ISIS, HORUS, *etc. sit on the throne surrounded by assorted mortals who dance as drums and music rise and lights go to out.*)

THE END

Black Lily and White Lily
Top: Gertrude E. Baker, Bottom: Kim Corbin
Photo by Roberta Barnes

Black Lily and
White Lily

Black Lily and White Lily

Black Lily and White Lily was first presented on January 5, 1996, as part of the 14th Annual New Plays Festival at Cleveland Public Theatre, Cleveland, Ohio, with the following cast:

Sue Johnson   Lily Mae
Beverly Young Wykoff   Lily Winslow

Directed by Nancy Burkinshaw

Black Lily and White Lily was revived as part of the One Two Three festival of one-act plays at the Guadalupe Cultural Arts Center and Palo Alto College in 2003 with Pamela Slocum and Antoinette Winstead, directed by Ric Slocum.

Characters:

LILY MAE   African American maid, middle-aged
LILY WINSLOW   Wealthy White Woman

Prologue

(A pile of clothes spills out from an open suitcase. LILY MAE *is putting on a dress over her head at lights up.)*

LILY WINSLOW: That's it. Now turn around. (L.M. *moves.*) No, faster. Twirl around.

LILY MAE: Twirl around? *(She spins until almost dizzy.)*

L.W.: That's enough, now don't overdo it.

L.M.: I really like this color, Mrs. Winslow. It brings out my skin tone.

L.W.: Now, put on the jacket. Yes, and let it kind of fall off your shoulders, casual like. That's right. Now walk over there and turn around.

(L.M. *does action.*)

L.M.: Like this?

L.W.: That's enough now. Take it off. I don't want to look at it any more. It reminds me of something. Something . . .

L.M.: Something sad?

L.W.: Why no. Eh, something wonderful . . .

L.M.: Like what, if I may be so bold.

L.W.: Lily Mae, you know that a real lady never reveals all her secrets. Not even to her dearest friend.

L.M.: Am I your dearest friend?

L.W.: Well, I don't know who is if you're not. Why else would I be giving you all these lovely things? Yes, that dress is better. Turn, turn. I associate it with calmer memories.

L.M.: Didn't you wear this one to the Christmas Party at Seven Oaks?

L.W.: Indeed I did, and what a deadly dull evening that was. All those Macallisters and Mavericks looking down their long brown noses at me. Old money can be so mean sometimes.

L.M.: *(Puts on a flamboyant hat.)* Would you look at that, Miss Lily, sho nuff some hot stuff.

L.W.: That would knock their eyes out at Sunday service.

L.M.: This might be a little too sassy for church, better after six to a chic cocktail affair...

L.W.: Do you think I'm shallow?

L.M.: What do you mean . . .

L.W.: I mean, you know. Nothing. Well, I took this test in *McCall's Magazine* which revealed that, according to my low score I was quite a shallow person.

L.M.: Don't pay no attention to that stuff. They just selling something you don't need is all.

L.W.: Oh, you're right. You're right as usual. It must really bother you to be so right all the time.
(*L.M. concludes the dress up and stands in her slip as lights fade.*)

Scene 1

LILY MAE: (*A sturdy middle-aged African American woman adjusts her hat looking into mirror. She wears a 1950s-style tailored suit.*) Do you like the hat? It's a Lilly Daché, don't cha know. Just like the one Princess Grace Kelly wore on the cover of *Life* magazine. And this suit? Man-tailored elegance from Lili-Anne of California. It's kinda funny that they share the same first name, Lily. That's the name of the lady that gave them to me, and it's my first name too. We're about the same size, except she's a little bigger in the bust. Shoot! That's no hill for a stepper. (*Takes falsies out of handbag and places them in suit.*) There. Miss Lily never likes to wear things more than two or three times. Good thing she married Eugene Winslow, The Motel King. Being a millionaire, he could afford her taste in shopping. Miz Lily Winslow was an all right woman to work for most of the time. She was born poor as Job's turkey so she did have her funny little ways after she married money. But she would give me little raises ever so often, and me and Rayetta lived decent. Rayetta's my grown daughter. I damn near never had to buy clothes, except for underwear and stockings of course. Gene Winslow used to like looking at me in Miz Winslow's old clothes. Said I looked better in them than she did. He sure could talk! Just full of bull corn. Or as the ladies say these days, bullshit, may he rest in peace. I was disappointed when he left me out of his will. After 27 years of service caring for his wives, his son, washing and ironing and such. Listen! I'll tell you something that's for real. You find out a lot about folks when you do their washing; what they had to eat, to drink, whether they sweat or bleed, if their bowels are loose or tight. (*Pause*) But I think I know why he did it. Left me out of his will, I mean. He didn't want Miz Lily to suspect anything. About us, him, and me. You know. That we would get, so to speak, real close every once in a while. It wasn't no big thing really; he never forced me; some do I know. But I knew what was what, and he did too. The next day I would find a hundred dollars in my shoe, or in the pocket of my apron. It came in handy with a child growing up and such and no man of my own to speak of. I never speak of Rayetta's daddy who used to run the road with the Brotherhood of Sleeping Car Porters. One day when she was about six, he just kept on running. Course, Rayetta would never wear Miz Lily's old clothes like I could. She always had to have new. Rayetta never liked Miz Lily much. Never did. She got so mad when I told her about me and Old Man Winslow. She said I wasn't nothing but a common whore. I thought she would understand, us being more like sisters than mother and daughter. Lord knows, you try to do what's right. I don't think she's ever respected me after that. Lord, children are such awful things. But where would we be without them, I guess.

Scene 2
(LILY WINSLOW, *a 60-ish white lady of faded beauty reclines on a chaise lounge and stares at the audience for a long count.*)
LILY WINSLOW: No. I haven't forgotten what I want to say. I find sitting still to be the most underrated of activities. And sitting still is quite a triumph for me personally. Not fidgeting, not talking, and most important of all, not smoking! It was my maid who got me to stop. She threatened me and insulted me and otherwise psychologically tortured me until I didn't have much choice. I quit. Cold turkey. None of that tapering-off nonsense. My maid was so grateful. The house didn't stink and the sheer white curtains were actually white once more. So, I discovered that I am still capable of making someone a little happier even in my present state of dilapidation. That alone would have been reason enough to be off the things. I would never quit for health reasons. I know all about cancer. I am intimate with it. I spit in the face of cancer. Lung or throat or otherwise. My husband died of the stuff. Cigars. It started as a shiny little brown spot on his lower lip and spread rapidly, to his brain. It was awful. He even tried to light up a cigar in the oxygen tent. Even after his lip was removed. It wasn't pretty. I don't know what I would have done without Lily Mae's help and strength through it all. Lily Mae's my maid. The only maid I've ever had. She was with my husband's family for years, practically raised his son Leo when Leo's mother died. Yes, I was his second wife. The Second Mrs. Winslow. We met in Las Vegas about a hundred years ago. He was there at some real estate do, and I was working on the strip at the Sands as a showgirl, not a stripper as people love

to think. Stripping takes talent, and I have absolutely none, except a talent for walking and smiling in a bathing suit and high heels with ten pounds of pink rooster feathers piled on top of my head. Boy, he was a sweet talker! I mean, the honey fairly dripped. We fell in love after a fashion, he with my face and body, and me with his motels. He owned five of them then. In Phoenix, Tucson, El Paso, San Antonio, and Corpus Christi. Well, doncha know, he took me on a tour of all of them. When we got to San Antonio, we got married, and he gave me one for a wedding present. The Alamo-Tel. I still own it too, though it quit making money years ago, when they built I-10 on top of it. I'm not a sentimental person as a rule, but when I am, I like to swim in sentiment. We honeymooned in Acapulco, at the Acapulco Princess. I still have the ashtray. When we came back to San Antonio, he moved me into this house, here on Contour Drive, where I have lived ever since. Lily Mae was already here when I arrived. We got along famously from the first. Oh, she wasn't called "Lily Mae" back then. I had to add the "Mae." We couldn't very well both be called Lily now could we? Think of the confusion. I would call her Lily Mae, or just plain Mae in front of company. I don't think she liked it very much at first. But she got used to it over the years.

(*Lights out*)

Scene 3

(*Lights up on the two women watching TV. LILY W. is reclining holding remote control "clicker"; LILY M. is seated in a chair, snapping green beans into a bowl.*)

LILY W.: (*Clicks remote*) I hate Lucy in this period. This period when they went to Hollywood and every out-of-work actor in town made a guest appearance. Oh my God, Harpo Marx! Why do people find him funny? Do you think he's funny? I think it's rather sad, really. A poor mute with obviously deep, psychological problems. I can understand about Groucho, at least Groucho made funny cracks, but this one—dear Lord! Should I click him?

LILY M.: No ma'am. I like this part.

L.W.: Do you think I'm lazy?

L.M.: No Ma'am, I don't think you're lazy.

L.W.: Like Pearl Bailey used to say, "I ain't lazy, I was just born tired."

L.M.: That wasn't Pearl Bailey, that was . . .

L.W.: Gene Winslow used to say I was the laziest white woman he ever saw.

L.M.: What did he mean by that?

L.W.: What are you snappin' those beans for Lily Mae? Don't we have frozen?

L.M.: Probably so. I likes doing it. It's soothing. Snapping tender green beans. Just listen to that sweet little snap.

L.W.: (Reacting to TV.) Oh please! That does it. I'm clicking you Harpo.

L.M.: Go head on click him if you want to.

(TV changes to all black rap video.)

L.W.: What in the world? Just look at those children! (Pause) What in heaven's name are you snapping snap beans for? Don't tell me you've taken up cooking at this late juncture.

L.M.: Like I said. It soothes me. Anyhow, does it matter whether I've taken up cooking or not?

L.W.: Well, of course it doesn't. I was just curious; there's no need to get so damn snappish about it.

(Phone rings.)

L.M.: (Answers phone.) Winslow's residence. Oh, hello, hon. Unh huh. Unh huh. Not yet. No. I will! Unh huh. I know that, honey. 'Bye.

L.W.: Was that Rayetta?

L.M.: Unh huh. Yes.

L.W.: Is everything all right?

L.M.: Yes, fine; just fine. Mrs. Winslow. We need to have us a little talk.

L.W.: Oh good! I like talking.

L.M.: We have to turn off the television.

L.W.: Why? I can listen and talk at the same time.

L.M.: Fine. Suit yourself. Look. Look here Mrs. Winslow; I'm quitting. I'm giving my two weeks notice now and I . . .

L.W.: You're what . . .?

L.M.: . . . And I want . . . I would like as my severance pay a check for five thousand dollars.

L.W.: (Shuts off TV.) You can't quit on me. What am I supposed to do for help for the rest of my life? You know how my knees swell up to the size of honeydew melons! I'm helpless!

L.M.: Get yourself one of those strong young women from Mexico.

L.W.: But I don't speak Mexican! You don't understand. What am I supposed to do? (She wails.)

L.M.: For gosh sakes Mrs. Winslow, *Gone With the Wind* is over!
(*L.W. stops crying. Pause.*)
    It was a very long movie, but like all things, it eventually came to an end.

L.W.: If I remember my Emily Post correctly, severance pay is only paid when the employer voluntarily terminates the employee, and not the other way around.

L.M.: But after 27 years Mrs. Winslow, I . . .

L.W.: If I were to accept the terms of your resignation, notice I did say "if," what in the world would you do with five thousand dollars?

L.M.: Buy a bus.

L.W.: A bus . . .

L.M.: Yes ma'am; a bus.

L.W.: What sort of bus?

L.M.: A school bus.

L.W.: A school bus.

L.M.: That's right.

L.W.: But why? Why in the world would you want to drive a school bus full of howling rug rats?

L.M.: Not to drive it myself . . .

L.W.: Well that's a relief, anyway.

L.M.: You know how many churches there are around here? How many colored churches?

L.W.: Quite a few I would imagine . . .

L.M.: Yes ma'am, and they all have choirs; and they all go to other churches in other towns around here to sing and fellowship; and they all go to conventions and picnics and retreats and, well you see what I mean? Why would they want to make Mr. Greyhound richer, when I can make them a better price?

L.W.: I believe you are actually serious.

L.M.: I know how to work it; I know it would work! I'd hire me a good experienced road driver, and I'd handle the bookings, and the books and Rayetta would help of course . . .

L.W.: Of course, Rayetta . . .

L.M.: Well? What you say?

L.W.: After all these years you could leave me and this house, at your age, to go driving up and down the highway at all hours with a busload of psalm-singing sisters.

L.M.: Sounds like heaven to me . . .

L.W.: I just don't believe your nerve. After all I've done for you.

L.M.: Here we go . . .

L.W.: Given you the clothes off my back . . .

L.M.: Which meant nothing to you.

L.W.: Shared my home with you and my husband with you . . .

L.M.: What do you mean by that remark, pray tell?

L.W.: You know very well what I mean. Do you think I didn't know? Do you think he didn't tell me?

L.M.: He told you?

L.W.: I was his wife; of course he told me. Years ago. Do you think I care? I was glad to have him off me even for one night.

L.M.: He told you! My Lord! Don't you see? He disrespected both you and me, by telling you about it, that son of a bitch.

L.W.: How very tragic. How very very Southern Gothic tragedy!

L.M.: *(Sobs and blows her nose into tissue.)*

L.W.: For Pete's sake, what are you crying about? I'm the one should be crying. You expect me to pay you five thousand dollars for the privilege of leaving me high and dry after all these years, when you know I am practically an invalid; and you know how hard it is to break in good help in this day and age. Do you think I was born yesterday morning?

L.M.: I'll help you find good help . . .

L.W.: You just think about this for a minute. Think about somebody beside yourself for a minute. Without you I would have to let myself go completely to hell, I believe I would.

L.M.: Mrs. Winslow please . . .

L.W.: Who else do I see, besides you? Who else do I see? Who? No one to be beautiful for . . . ever again. Never again . . . *(She sobs melodramatically.)*

L.M.: That won't work Mrs. Winslow. That "guilt" stuff.

L.W.: And why not? It's been working for thousands of years.

L.M.: Do you really think the slave chooses his chains?

L.W.: I don't think anything. I don't think about it! *(Pause)* But, since you seem determined to go, I will write you a check for five thousand dollars.

L.M.: Thank you, Jesus!

L.W.: But I do so not as "severance pay," which is absurd, but as a little business loan, which you must pay back with interest.

L.M.: *(Handing L.W. her pocketbook.)* That's fine. I'll make the payments. Make it out in Rayetta's name.

L.W.: *(Writing check.)* . . . And I do so for one reason and for one reason only which has nothing to do with me wanting to finance you in some "I Love Lucy" scheme that is, no doubt, doomed to failure, as well as requiring me to deprive myself of your irreplaceable service.

L.M.: Yes ma'am, I hate to do it but . . . what reason?

L.W.: It will be worth the pleasure I will feel, when you come crawling back to me, and I will then be able to utter the most satisfying words in the English language. I. Told. You. So.

(Hands check to L.M. She kisses it.) (Lights out)

Scene 4

(L.M. is dressed as in Scene 1, addresses audience.)

L.M.: Suddenly, there I was: an entrepreneur! Business was real good that first summer. The National Baptist Convention was in Austin that year, and I took up three full loads in nine hours going and coming. I made a little over seven hundred dollars, after I'd paid my expenses. I stayed up there that whole weekend shuttling the folks from the hotel to the various churches in town: Ebenezer, Brown's Chapel, First Baptist, Second Baptist, Mt. Zion, Mt. Shiloh, Mt. Sinai, Mt. Calvary, Mt. Olive, and the rest. At each church, I passed out cards and drummed up more business. I was a natural-born businesswoman, which seemed to surprise everyone but me. How'd they think I ran the Winslows' house all them years? By hook or crook? I opened up two or three charge accounts, put me a down payment on a new little Chevrolet, even paid old lady Winslow a few payments back, much to her surprise. Yes, I was living the American dream sure enough. And then the incident, as it came to be called, took place—out on Highway 10, just outside of Ft. Stockton, which was our rest stop between here and El Paso. We were coming back from the Eastern Star spring retreat, which was held in El Paso that year. Did I say that already? Rayetta says I tend to repeat myself like an old lady, but what can you expect, know what I mean? Anyway, the incident, as it happened, was not the result of too much beer drinking and a weak bladder, as the gossip goes. Unh uh. It was just old Mr. Mulkey, in confusion, and the fact that he had lost his eyeglasses, had simply relieved himself against the big back tire of the bus. Because he couldn't find the colored restroom, which of course had gone out of business years before; and he refused to use what he thought was the white restroom, which just said "Men" on the door. He got very agitated, as he explained it later, and his agitation put pressure on his bladder, so he couldn't hold it, so, well, he just went on an' urinated against the back tire. Poor thing. He was too near-sighted to see the mother and little daughter coming out of the Baskin-Robbins, or the highway patrolman just pulling in for a doughnut. He was just in time to see old Mr. Mulkey do his business, and hear the lady scream. He ran over and handcuffed Mr. Mulkey, and Mr. Mulkey started crying, thought they were gonna lynch him I expect. He tried to explain himself, but it was no use. It was terrible. Just terrible. The mamma screamed again and ran over all red-faced, telling the highway patrol that that old darkey had ruined her little daughter for life. Talking 'bout he shook his penis in her little pink face. He was just shaking off the last little drips, you know, the way men do so they don't stain their underwear. But God above knows, people see what they want to see; or what they NEED to see, which is even worse. Somehow it got into the newspapers down here; the *Express News* gave it a headline like it was World War III. "Local Flasher Terrorizes Ft. Stockton," or some such thing. Well. That was the end of my touring bus business. I had to pay Mr. Mulkey's bail, then his legal fees and fine. The judge thought $1,000 and ten years probation was about fair for such a terrible crime. On top of that, I got sued by Baskin-Robbins people. Said their business was ruined when the story got around. Shoot; THEIR business. My insurance was cancelled. You can't transport people without insurance, you know. That was that. I sold the bus. What else could I do? I took a little loss on it all, I admit that, but I still had my health, right? Anything is possible if you got your health.

(*Lights go down*)

Scene 5

(*Lights up on L.W. She is as before, but now, a bit disheveled, newspapers, pop bottles, and assorted trash are about her on the floor. After a pause she speaks.*)

L.W.: I had a rather disturbing meditation this afternoon. Sometimes when I'm sitting, just holding still, like I like to do, the stillness produces phenomena out of itself—sometimes monsters, sometimes angels, sometimes a clear white light. This afternoon, a face came to me out of the stillness, just as clear as anything . . . my mother's face. My old mother looking for all the world like she did the day she dropped dead after not being sick a day in her life. Stroke, they said. Massive. Went like THAT. She was an elementary school teacher in Louisiana, poor thing, and she dropped dead in September of 1955—the year that *Brown v. Board of Education* took effect. My dear mother, for some reason, just hated the colored. Just hated them. Like ice. It didn't matter to her how nice any of them were, or clean and polite. *Brown v. Board of Education* was the Supreme Court decision that integrated the public schools in the South, starting with the first grade. My dear mother had taught first grade for over forty years. Some said she died of a broken heart. She used to tell me when I was a little girl: "Now Lillian, you just cannot let your inferior races get any idea that they're as good as us. Once you open that door, even a crack, there'd be no turning back. It's like wiping your behind on a wagon wheel; there's just no end to it." In the middle of my meditation this afternoon, my mother's face smiled at me, like she was just right above my head looking down. Mother almost never smiled, but sure enough, there she was, just smiling away. She was holding a little Bible which she opened to a verse I had never heard before. It read: beware ye the underdog, for he giveth a deadly bite. *(Phone rings. She answers it.)* Hello? Oh, hello stranger? Has the Baptist church made you a millionaire yet? What? Why yes, of course you can come over. I would love to talk to you as always. 'Bye. *(She hangs up and tidies-up as best she can without leaving the chaise. After a moment, LILY MAE appears at her doorway, carrying a small suitcase.)*

L.M.: I'm back.

L.W.: So I see. Come in, come in; we're not strangers, are we? *(L.M. takes a few steps in.)* My knees have gone down quite a bit, since the last time you were here. Did you notice?

L.M.: They look about the same to me, Mrs. Winslow.

L.W.: Well they're not. They've gone down quite a bit. I didn't imagine it.

L.M.: No ma'am, I guess you didn't. How's the new woman doing?

L.W.: What new woman? Oh, her. I had to fire her. Weeks ago. A thief I can stand, but a liar, never! I've managed quite all right by myself. I think.

L.M.: Yes, I can see that you have.

L.W.: *(Pause)* Well . . .?

L.M.: Well . . . Mrs. Winslow, I would like my old position back if . . .

L.W.: I don't mean that, silly! Well, didn't you miss me?

L.M.: I suppose I did, miss you, in a manner of speaking.

L.W.: I knew you would. And I missed you too, Lily Mae. Well course you can have your old job back.

L.M.: Ain't you going to say it?

L.W.: Say what?

L.M.: You know. The most powerful words in the English language . . .

L.W.: No. No, I'm not. Now that you're really here, I take no pleasure in humiliating you. I'm just glad to see you. And to know that things turned out all right. I feel sorry for you. I actually do. Come on in and rest your handbag. *(L.M. does so.)* Turn on the television *(She does.)* And give me a little neck rub will you please. *(She begins massage.)* Nobody has hands like yours . . .

L.M.: I still intend to pay you back all you loaned me. With interest, but it'll have to be a little at a time, but you know I'm good for it, even if it takes . . . *(L.W. bursts out laughing.)*

L.W.: Oh, Lily Mae, Lily Mae! I guess I can tell you now. Ha Ha! Life is really so funny. Know what I mean, so flat-out funny!

L.M.: Tell me what? What's funny?

L.W.: You don't have to pay me back at all. Not one nickel, not one penny . . .!

L.M.: Don't play with my nerves, now. Tell me what you mean.

L.W.: I mean it was your money all along. Isn't that great?

L.M.: What do you mean, "mine"?

L.W.: I mean yours, silly Mae. Gene Winslow left it you in his will, five thousand dollars, exactly. I was his executrix, of course, and I just never bothered to tell you about it; just kept it between me and my attorneys. I figured I'd give it to you some day, if you were a good girl. And I did give it to you. I actually did. Isn't life funny?

L.M.: Why . . .? Why . . .?

L.W.: As I remember, I was a little p.o.'ed at you, right after the old man died. You going around acting more like the widow than me. I grieved too. I just grieved in my own way. I intended to give it to you someday. And after a while, it slipped my mind. And then you asked me for it. Ha! Isn't it funny the way life turns out.

(Massage continues.)

L.M.: Do you know how easy it would be to kill you, right now? To take your windpipe between my thumbs, and just snap?

(Lights start down)

L.W.: Stop. Stop it! Now! *(Lights out)* You're tickling me, Lily Mae! Lily M. . . .!!!

THE END

Miranda Rites
L-R: Bonnie Victor Fried and Veronica Gonzales
Photo by Roberta Barnes

Miranda Rites

Miranda Rites: A Spirit Play

Miranda Rites was first presented on November 25, 1994, by Jump-Start Performance Company, with the following cast:

Bonnie Victor Fried	Martha Mitchell
Toni Marsh	1st Nurse/Dorothy Dandridge
Veronica Gonzales	Dr. Montalvo/Carmen Miranda
Deborah Basham-Bums	2nd Nurse/Marilyn Monroe

Directed by Arnold Aprill
Production Design by Robert Rehm
Lighting Design by Steve Bailey
Arnold Aprill, Dramaturg
Written in collaboration with Arnold Aprill

Characters:

FIRST NURSE/DOROTHY DANDRIDGE
   African American in her 30s
SECOND NURSE/ MARILYN MONROE/JOHN MITCHELL
   Blonde, mid-30s
DR. MONTALVO/CARMEN MIRANDA
   Latina, attractive, efficient
MARTHA MITCHELL
   Brassy, fiftyish Southern belle

Prologue

(MARTHA *is on the phone talking to an old friend.*)
MARTHA: They needn't have gone to all that trouble to kill me, you know. I wanted to die. I really did. I've attempted suicide on a regular basis over the past few years, but have so far succeeded only in killing myself by painful inches. Once I knew I was dying, hell, it was a relief. No more worrying about bills, the press, my hair, the decline of American life. What's death to a Christian, anyway, but endless peace after a lifetime of suffering? And what woman has suffered more than me? My husband doesn't love me, I mean, my "ex." The bastard. He's turned my own child against me. Maybe I could have done better by her, but she doesn't understand the constant pressure of being in the national spotlight. I see it all so clearly now that all the cards are on the table. I begged him to move back with me to 5th Avenue, where we could live like normal people. I told him point-blank I would leave him if he didn't. And I meant it. It was Mr. President or me. He made his choice as you know, and now I'm in the cold without a pot to pee in. The downright cruelty of it. The bastard has cut off my MasterCards and all accounts. Yes, I have my own money, several thousands at home in Pine Bluff. I'd get it out in a minute if I could remember the name of the bank. I'm losing my mind along with everything else. Meanwhile, I have to beg for groceries, when I'm strong enough to eat. I have no man to care for me. I, who collected men's hearts like butterflies. Disappointed? I'll say, I'm utterly disappointed, and who wouldn't be, in my shoes! No, you have been a true friend, for sticking by me but the rest of the so-called loyal and true leave quite a bit to be desired in the fidelity department. O.K. well, call me back later, you know how nervous I get without a phone in my hand. 'Bye. (*She hangs up phone, takes out a cigarette and lights it, dials a number.*) Hello, yourself; it's Martha. Yes, you know, they needn't have gone to such a fuss to kill me; I was ready to die, yes; it's a big load off my mind, if they only knew . . . (*Lights down*)

ACT ONE

(*A hospital room with a single bed. The bed is covered by a gauze curtain. The room is dim. A NURSE enters and opens the window blinds. She pulls back the curtain on the bed. MARTHA is lying in it wearing a sleep mask. She is very still. NURSE reads chart at the foot of her bed.* MARTHA *stirs, and removes mask from her eyes.)*

NURSE: How are we doing this morning?

MARTHA: I don't know about you, but I feel like shit warmed over. What time is it?

NURSE: Almost seven. Time for breakfast. Today is pearl tapioca day. If you're a good girl.

MARTHA: Just bring me some black coffee and a couple of doughnuts, if you please. And close those blinds. My eyes are killing me.

NURSE: Did you sleep well?

MARTHA: No. I have bad dreams. Terrible. I've had 'em ever since I was attacked.

NURSE: Why would anyone want to attack you? (*Begins taking* MARTHA's *vital signs; blood pressure, temperature, etc., during following.)*

MARTHA: Three guesses and the first two don't count.

NURSE: Are you taking your medication?

MARTHA: Of course I am. I'm paying for it; I'll take it. What happened to the other nurse? The mousy one.

NURSE: She's off duty. I'm Nurse Harris. I'm taking care of you for a while.

MARTHA: Where's my doctor?

NURSE: Making the rounds. Don't worry; he'll get to you as soon as he can.

MARTHA: You're colored, aren't you?

NURSE: Equal opportunity health care providers. That's our motto.

MARTHA: My mother would have a shit-fit, God rest her soul. I don't know why, since colored have nursed white since time immemorial.

NURSE: Probably before that even . . .

MARTHA: You all take care of white folks better than you do your own families. Don't get me wrong. The public has an awful misconception about us Republicans. We're the party of Lincoln, remember?

(2ND NURSE brings in food tray and places it on the bed. She spills the juice on the tray: "Oops! Sorry!" and clumsily wipes it up. 2ND NURSE exits.)

MARTHA: You expect me to eat this stuff? It has no flavor at all.

NURSE: Be nice, Mrs. Mitchell. You have to eat. Or, we'll have to give you a high colonic.

MARTHA: You do, and I'll sue this hospital and have you arrested for statutory rape! *(DR. MONTALVO enters. She is a sleek professional with glasses and tailored suit.)* Just see if I don't!

DR.: What's all the excitement?

MARTHA: Who in the Sam Hill are you?

DR.: *(NURSE shows chart to DR.)* I'm Dr. Montalvo. That will be all. Thank you, nurse. *(NURSE exits.)* I came to see if you're feeling better today, if you've been having those funny dreams again.

MARTHA: I already have a doctor, thank you. I'll just wait and talk to him, if you don't mind.

DR.: He asked me to come and meet you, Mrs. Mitchell.

MARTHA: Ah really? How do I know you're not some FBI goon? What are you writing? Let me see . . .!

DR.: Just notes of what you say. See? Nothing more. You're the talk of the hospital, you know. We don't get many celebrities here.

MARTHA: I don't give out autographs anymore, so don't ask. No telling where it might end up.

DR.: I don't want your autograph. Do you think everyone you meet wants something from you?

MARTHA: No, not everyone, just you.

DR.: I see. *(She writes in notebook.)*

MARTHA: I must be insane. Insanely naive. The irony alone could drive you mad! Ha! Ha! Ha! I hope you're getting all this down for the book you'll be writing to exonerate the FBI, after I'm dead.

DR.: Why would the FBI send me to spy on you? All they'd have to do is wiretap the walls.

MARTHA: I have ugly nightmares.

DR.: Tell me.

MARTHA: Dreams that make me sweat . . .

DR.: What happens in these dreams?

MARTHA: Oh no, it's not that easy. My dreams aren't for publication.

DR.: Not for publication. For interpretation. Do you know the story of the little boy who cried wolf?

MARTHA: What? That's old wives' talk.

DR.: Quite a few folk tales have a basis in psychological truth.

MARTHA: You're losing me, Doc.

DR.: Honesty is the best policy, isn't it?

MARTHA: Depends on who you ask.

DR.: I'd like to hypnotize you. Would you mind?

MARTHA: Ha, that would be quite a task, since I'm already hypnotized with fear and boredom . . .

93

DR.: It would relax you.

MARTHA: I'm not tense. I just woke up. You want to pick my brains while I'm defenseless, and I know it.

DR.: You must know there are parties, certain parties, who, shall we say, have a vested interest in maintaining deniability.

MARTHA: I know, I know! Certain parties have gone to great lengths to prove I'm crazy! Crazy Martha, and her crazy dreams. But I'll tell you one thing; I know the difference between dreams and reality, even when I'm asleep!

DR.: Everything you say will be completely off the record.

MARTHA: I've heard that before . . .

DR.: There are things I must know in order to diagnose you properly, to fully explore your paranoia. Nobody wants to hurt you, you know.

MARTHA: Go on, do your stuff. Just don't make me cluck like a chicken or some damn thing.

DR.: You have my word on it. Look into this light, please, Martha. And think of nothing but soft black. Your mind is clear of worry and pain. You are relaxed and trust in the face value of vacant consciousness. Are you totally relaxed, Martha?

MARTHA: Totally re . . . lax . . .

DR.: Good. Now, you will cluck like a chicken. (MARTHA *responds.*) That's good. Follow the sound of my voice, as it gets lower, and lower, you will go back in time. The deeper my voice the farther back in your memory we will go.

MARTHA: O.K. (*She gets up and grabs a phone receiver and a glass of scotch.*) Things are going on in Washington that would curl your hair. Dirty things, Maxine, dirty at the highest level. It makes me so goddamn mad; Mr. President has tricked him, dirty-tricked my husband the Attorney General of the United States, into breaking the law of the land. Law and order. Ha! Don't make me laugh if you know what's good for you. No, I said tricked, tricked! I can't talk louder, the walls have ears and the phones are tapped. Dirty track-covering tricks. Who do you think? My husband has his faults, but he understands the U.S. Constitution; he would never pull off such a stunt by himself. It was Mr. President himself planned the whole thing. No; the WHOLE thing, from breaking into Daniel Ellsberg's psychiatrist's office and everything that came before and after, that's what. To get proof. Proof that the liberal communists had infiltrated the DNC and were ready to hand the government over to the Russians. They had proof but they were greedy for more. Maxine, I tell you the monkeyshines have been going on for years, but as a rule they are not so goddamn stupid enough to get caught red-handed. I tell you, I could make you cry with the information that I've been exposed to. I told my husband, get out of Washington, out of politics before it sucks you dry. The trail has been sniffed out, and it leads clear up Pennsylvania Avenue. If Mr. President had any guts at all, which we can discuss later, he would resign at once and save the nation a lot of grief. Where am I? That's a real good question, because it's not so much where I am as why. I'm hiding in the back room of a hotel suite in California, and I have been cut off from anything happening in Washington at all, so Mr. President and my husband can plan the cover-up without any interference from me. Oh God, Maxine! Help call the police. Call . . . Stop it! You . . .! Help me! He . . . No, NO!

(Enter DR. MONTALVO who has transformed into CARMEN. She is dancing to samba music. She is wearing traditional Bahian "tutti frutti" costume. Lights down on CARMEN and up on MARTHA sitting up in hospital bed. From the darkness emerge two insect-like government agents played by the NURSES, but wearing black shades. They slowly approach MARTHA and begin injecting her with giant hypodermic needles. CARMEN and NURSES exit.)

MARTHA: *(sings)*
A funny thing happened to me on the way to the grave—
Can a small town girl save herself
And save her country?
When I tell the truth, why do they say:
It's just that crazy Martha. She's off her head.
Maybe she'd be better off dead.
There is a cancer growing on the presidency,
More evil than the strange malignancy
Growing in me.
Now is the time for all good women
To leave the country club or be prepared
To leave the country.
Tonight I'm in a restless mood
Bored out of my mind, crazed with hunger
From not eating this hospital food
And why do they keep it so cold in here?
Do they think I'm already dead?

My friends never call
They're probably all
On the FBI's payroll.
And they never once in all these many years
Refused an invitation to the many parties I gave!
I have to laugh, ha ha, because
A very funny thing happened to me
On the way to the grave.

(MARTHA *is weeping quietly until she sees* CARMEN. CARMEN *watches for a moment and then enters area.*)

MARTHA: What in the Sam Hill are you doing here?

CARM.: Relax, sister. I'm Carmen Miranda, the Tutti Frutti Angel of Death. *(Pause)* I've come to read you your rights . . .

MARTHA: My husband was Attorney General of the United States of America, God help us, so I would just watch my mouth, if I was you, missy.

CARM.: Your husband the Attorney General is doing time up the river. Do not threaten me with your corrupt influences, or I will be forced to turn your face to stone.

MARTHA: Yeah? Just try it.

CARM.: Or perhaps I shall make your tongue swell to the size of a football, causing your jaw to disconnect at its hinges; would you like that?

MARTHA: Now I know I'm dreaming. It's that dope those big nurses shot me up with. Ow! What was it, anyway? I feel just awful. My arms feel like pincushions!! My arms! Look what they did; these bruises, these puncture marks from sucking out my blood. What are they going to do with all that blood, tell me that? Pour it over vanilla ice cream and eat it for dessert?!

CARM.: Stop acting so crazy; you're as sane as I am.

MARTHA: I hate this place. I never get my phone messages. I've told people to call me twice a day every day, but do they do it? Three guesses and the first two don't count. It's a wonder I'm not crazy as a bedbug.

CARM.: I've come to take you away from all that; your arms, your husband, everything.

MARTHA: Good. I'm about ready to go, too. Poor John is quite doomed without me, I'm afraid. I knew when I married him that he was—flawed.

CARM.: Flawed?

MARTHA: He figured out how to accomplish, to achieve . . .

CARM.: . . . But he never felt he deserved it so he always screwed himself in the ass without K.Y., so to speak.

MARTHA: My, you do have a filthy mouth. What are you? Some sort of she-devil?

CARM.: Not even.

MARTHA: That's good. I do not want to go to hell, believe me, because I do not tan. I burn like a biscuit.

CARM.: You have the right to remain silent . . .

MARTHA: What? Silent! Ha! Ha! Funny girl. The liberal communists want me to remain silent, the liberal communists and the left-wing Nazis that have gotten themselves into government service. Silence equals tyranny, and tyranny is worse than death. The grave is silent soon enough.

CARM.: I've come to take you through that door.

MARTHA: Say! Are you really Carmen Miranda, or just some actress in a Carmen Miranda outfit?

CARM.: The real Carmen Miranda was just some actress in a Carmen Miranda outfit! How real do you want to get, really?

(Sound of bells)

MARTHA: What is that bell tolling for?

CARM.: Visiting hours.

MARTHA: What?

CARM.: Visiting hours have begun. After visiting hours are over, you must come with me, O.K.?

MARTHA: I don't want visitors! I want to go home to die like a civilized American citizen.

CARM.: It doesn't matter where you die. I'm going now to make my rounds.

MARTHA: Rounds?

CARM.: When I return, you must come with me.

MARTHA: I heard you the first time. I'm not retarded, you know. *(CARMEN goes.) (MARTHA takes a cigarette from under her pillow and lights it.) (Knock at door. She puts cigarette out.)* What now. *(MARILYN MONROE enters.)*

MARIL.: Hello, Martha. I came over to cheer you up. I'm still working on my sadness problem, every chance I get.

MARTHA: Marilyn Monroe! Marilyn Monroe! Good lord, am I as dead as you?

MARIL.: Hold on, neither of us is exactly dead, in the broadest sense.

MARTHA: Is that supposed to make me feel better?

MARIL.: Being dead isn't so bad. It's simply the loss of incandescence.

MARTHA: What are you going on about? Iridescence?

MARIL.: Incandescence, I said.

MARTHA: You're not as dumb as you act, sometimes. Say! JFK never loved you! But, Bobby did. Bobby was an honest-to-god lover boy. And his daddy's little spoiled brat darling baby, too.

MARIL.: He took on Hoover for me, you know J. Edgar, King of the Closet Queens Hoover, just because they insulted me. Dishonored my name.

MARTHA: What do you mean?

MARIL.: Don't you know what honor is?

MARTHA: I know what it is, all right. My husband thought he practically invented the concept; he said the word "honor" at least three times before he took his morning crap.

MARIL.: You're just in a bad mood because you're going to die soon.

MARTHA: My mood as you call it, results from the fact that I was never sick a day in my life, before this business. They knew that it would be impossible to shut me up. So they did the next best thing. They destroyed my credibility as a sane caring person. And when I still got press coverage, they decided to give me this weird disease that no one's ever heard of. They hate me because I saw it all, not just Watergate, but the connection between everything and everything else.

MARIL.: Saw what?

MARTHA: The connection. The connection between Watergate, and the murder of those Kennedy boys, whose approval you so desperately craved; and the death of Martin Luther King, Malcolm X, the Bay of Pigs, Mai Lai, the assassination of Salvador Allende and the relationship between the Brazilian rainforests and the Big Mac, the creation of an economy driven by dope and guns, re-enforced by . . .

MARIL.: Look, I came to cheer you up. I don't care what you've done; but if that's the kind of thing you've been saying, it's a wonder they haven't killed you sooner.

MARTHA: . . . The connection between the assassination of Abraham Lincoln and the death of Emmitt Till.

MARIL.: Who? No, don't tell me.

MARTHA: Now, they've seen to it that I become more and more disconnected from any connections at all, with . . .

MARIL.: I came to cheer you up. Shall I sing you a song?

MARTHA: Good Lord, no. Tell me a story. A funny one.

MARIL.: O.K. Let's see. Oh yeah, I was born into a broken home . . .

MARTHA: Oh that story cracks me up! Ha! Ha! Don't stop . . .

MARIL.: My mother lost her mind when I was two, and I was passed around.

MARTHA: Stop! This part kills me! Ha! Go on! Go on!!

MARIL.: . . . From foster home to orphanage; as an innocent child, I was used as a sexual toilet.

MARTHA: You're tickling me to death, now . . .!

MARIL.: I grew wise; I grew bitter . . .

MARTHA: Stop it, please! I can't stand it . . .

MARIL.: I gave Carl Sandburg head. I'm not sorry about it. I'm glad. Don't I deserve to live in the White House? I came this close to toppling a dynasty.

MARTHA: You were only capable of toppling yourself. It toppled anyway, without your assistance, a few short years later, as history knows.

MARIL.: History has a way of rewriting itself. But there are things, parts of it that will never be written, much less, rewritten. Only hinted at. Whispered.

MARTHA: That's what keeps the lid on. Silence. Silence is golden. Well, so what? So is pee. Silence is deadly as the poison shot into my veins by those mean nurses. They are not nice people! I keep telling them to get me a telephone; they just ignore me. Like I was a child with a fever. I know you have this room bugged, so listen up, you pigs. I don't mind dying; everybody has to do it. But at least find me a working telephone before I die of boredom! I wish John would call, the sorry son of a bitch. How many days have I been here?

MARIL.: Too many, I'm afraid. Things have been set in motion. You know.

(DOROTHY DANDRIDGE *enters dressed as Carmen Jones, holding a tray with a telephone and a bud vase with a single carnation.*)

DOT.: (*Singing to herself*) You go for me! And I'm Tabu . . .!

MARTHA: What do you want? Is that a trick phone? A prop phone?

DOT.: Try it and see.

MARTHA: (*Picks up phone and dials.*) Busy! This thing is no good. (*She slams down phone.*) Take it back, and that stinking carnation too. Carnations are for cheap funerals. My burial will be very elaborate; with pink gladiolus and white roses for sorrow.

DOT.: Hello Miss Baker, and I don't mean Josephine . . .

MARIL.: Dorothy Dandridge, dead and among us again. I didn't know you had an interest in this case.

DOT.: I haven't worked in so long, you know, and I sniffed a good part for a tragic mulatto. I smell tragedy the way some folks smell fried chicken.

MARIL.: Why the Carmen Jones drag? A little dated, isn't it?

DOT.: Yeah, like you would have recognized me without it.

MARIL.: There's only one real Carmen in this opera, and it ain't the factory girl . . .

DOT.: Believe me, I am NOT after her job. I'm strictly a volunteer, like you.

MARTHA: There's more to it than that. God, don't tell me that John Kennedy was drilling you too!

DOT.: He was NOT. Though you're getting warm.

MARTHA: John Kennedy masterminded his own assassination to get power in the underworld. Not many people know that.

MARIL.: That's crazy. Oswald killed Kennedy.

DOT.: Yeah, Oswald the Rabbit.

MARIL.: Wait! Fidel. It was Fidel, wasn't it!

MARTHA: Fidel killed Kennedy?

DOT.: Fidel was deeply in love with me.

MARIL.: Yeah, he thought you were Carmen Jones. Peter Lawford told me all about it.

DOT.: The FBI had bugs all over my house, by my pool. They tailed me for years, as they did every Negro in the country who talked back . . .till it became impossibly expensive. By that time, I had a white husband, and started my spiral down the spiral staircase of booze and depression. Then the press started in on me like I was the slut of Babylon. Assaulted my dignity in the most vulnerable places.

MARTHA: What a waste of taxpayers' money.

MARIL.: Is that why you killed yourself?

DOT.: It didn't help.

MARTHA: Why are you two tragic divas trying to cheer me up? It isn't working. I'm going to cry in a minute.

(*Lights change to '40s spy movie lighting, black and white, slow samba music.*)

DOT.: J. Edgar Hoover wanted me to poison Fidel. He planted heroin on me, and then threatened me with exposure. I had no real choice. I got myself invited deep sea fishing on his yacht. During dinner he never took his eyes off me. I had the poison in a locket around my neck. One drop was enough to cause instant subdurat hematoma. The moon rose on the waters of the bay, as a samba band called everyone to dance. I knew he would be napping in his cabin as was his habit before the evening's serious partying. I opened the door to his cabin . . . there he was; all six-foot-three of his glorious manhood stretched on the bed before me, wearing nothing but his beard and a smile. I walked toward the bed. He opened his eyes slightly. "I've been expecting you," he says softly in Spanish, holding out his hand to me. I could not bring myself to kill such a beautiful man. Besides, I don't kill for governments. *(Lights return to normal.)*

MARIL.: Wow! If you'd had dialogue like that in your films, you would've been a big movie star instead of a . . .

DOT.: A what? A Mulatta Exotica Neurotica?

MARIL.: Gee, you're sensitive. It must have been really hard for you, being beautiful and brown in an ugly white business.

DOT.: You said a mouthful. High yellow beauty was a curse in this line of work. I'm classy and educated too. What was my mother thinking? She said I could compete with Ava Gardner and Yvonne de Carlo for a variety of leading lady roles. White and Negro men would fantasize about me equally. And they did. For a while. But that was all. I was as forbidden to one as to the other, you know. Too black to be white, too white to be black. Too beautiful to work. Too beautiful to live.

MARIL.: I'm sorry.

MARTHA: Hold it. I am the patient here, if you please. I will not allow you two vivid hallucinations to steal from me what is essentially a one-woman show! That's better. Stand together so I can see both of you without breaking my neck off. Good. Now, I have a couple of questions for you two gals.

MARIL.: Questions? Is that in our contracts?

DOT.: Shoot. Ask away.

MARTHA: First off, that Death number: is it really necessary?

BOTH: YES.

DOT.: Next question?

MARTHA: Can we just get down to it, please?

MARIL.: Ask away!

DOT.: Shoot your shot.

MARTHA: What did the President know, and when did he know it?

(MARIL. *takes phone, dials, and hands it to* MARTHA. *She listens for a second and then speaks.*)

MARTHA: Hello, Marty? It's me, your MOTHER. Marty, don't start that crying, I'm not dead YET? Marty, if you don't quit it this minute, I'm going to hang up the phone; big girls don't cry, I mean it! I didn't call you up to listen to you crying tears of guilt. I really mean it, Marty, just stop it. What? How should I know? They keep me so doped up all the time I don't know whether I'm awake or asleep half the time. I just get sicker and sicker every day; not that I'm surprised. Pain? Yes, I have pains. I am a mass of pains. Wild dogs are chewing on my nerves, if you really want to know the truth; but that's not why I called. Listen. Listen! I can't get through to your father! Not the White House, you ninny! OUR house on 5th Avenue. I can't reach my home. Be a dear and try it for me will you? Those FBI geniuses have no doubt screwed up the phone lines. Just try it. Try it for me, and tell John to get me out of here at once. I know he hates me, but he couldn't hate me that much, could he? I'm afraid. I'm afraid to die here. Lord knows what they'll do to my parts. Tell John it's urgent, you hear me? God, don't you know the number?! It's . . . it's 761-787776, oh no; 767-77077. Oh God, Marty, look it up, can't you? Just do it now. Don't start the bawling again, I mean it! I'll hang up this phone! O.K., O.K., I'm warning you . . . (*She slams phone down.*) Hell. (*Lights a cigarette. She gets out of bed and goes to the window. Music up.*)

(Sings)

Without a man
What is a woman but a person
Trying to get by as best she can?
Never looking too long in the mirror
Never seeing the fear near and dear in the eyes
Of her fortunate friends.
"Poor thing," their eyes whisper,
Too bad you'll be dying
Alone, later on this year, we fear,
Without a man,
To at least make arrangements and
Mourn in a dignified way, and to generously
Pay for the flowers and catering

After you're planted away.
What a sad sad day to be without a man.
DOT.: *(Special on DOROTHY)*
Without a man
What is a woman
But the best of all possible worlds rolled into one!
Well equipped with the power and knowledge and
Grace to get by
Without diamonds or pearls; but unwilling to go
Without mutual love
And respect for who she is, standing alone in the world
With or without a man.
(Lights down)
MARIL.: *(Special on MARIL.)*
Without a man
What is a woman
But a distinguished actress
Playing Maggie the Cat or Antigone
Without using extra Max Factor on a black and blue cheekbone
That recently got in the way of the back of
His swinging right hand.
My hair would go back to its natural color,
Sort of a deep tawny tan.
In the world that I think about, dream about;
Without a man.
(Lights down)
MARTHA: Men; you can't live with 'em, and you can't live WITH
'em. All I know is, without one, life would degenerate into a
never-ending slumber party. That's not my cup of tea.
(Sings)
Without a man
What is a woman
To do but to try not to cry growing bitter and dry,
Getting by with a sigh and a couple of pills.
Your advice, though quite nice, won't suffice 'cause
I simply don't understand how you can imagine paradise
Without a man.
DOR.: I can.
MARIL.: I can...
BOTH: It's easy.
ALL: Without a man.

(Lights change)
(Samba music. CARMEN *enters as music continues.* MARILYN *and* DOROTHY *minister to* MARTHA *in bed with sharp instruments. They attach tubes to her arms and legs and begin manipulating her like a marionette.)*
MARTHA: Wait! *(To* CARM.*)* I'm not ready for you yet!
CARMEN: Don't worry, Chica. This is merely a musical interlude, nothing to do with you. *(Sings)*
I have the kind of beauty
To take away your breath!
I am the Tutti Frutti
Angel of Death!
From South of the Border
That's where I get my style
From too much information
That's where I get my smile

Ayi yi yi yi yi yi yi yi F B ayi!
Dancing underneath a Tropicana sky
Si si si si si si si si si C I A!
Always preserve the power
To deny!
(She is joined by DOROTHY *and* MARILYN *dressed in "fruit salad" headdresses and playing maracas. Song repeats with all three singing and dancing around* MARTHA's *bed.* MARTHA *rises and dances with them, dragging the I.V. tubes and apparatus with her.)*
I am that special cutie
I take away your breath!
I am the Tutti Frutti
Angel of Death!
From South of the Border
That's where I get my style
From too much information
That's where I get my smile

Ayi yi yi yi yi yi yi yi F B ayi!
Dancing underneath a Tropicana sky
Si si si si si si si si si C I A!
Always preserve the power
To deny!

(At song's end, CARMEN *exits,* MARTHA *gets back in bed.* MARILYN *and* DOROTHY *sit on either side of the bed.* DOT. *is reading a gossip magazine, and* MARIL. *is buffing her nails.* MARTHA *has her eyes closed. After a moment she opens them and looks at her visitors.)*
MARTHA: God. Are you broads still here?
DOT.: You dozed off.
MARTHA: Visiting hours must surely be over . . .
MARIL.: It's the Nembutal. It makes reality go in and out like the tide.
DOT.: Where do they get this stuff? Does anybody believe it?
MARIL.: Everybody does. What does it say about you?
DOT.: . . . Says I'm a threat to national security.
MARIL.: National security! That's a laugh. I breached national security so many times it would make your head swim.
MARTHA: My head is swimming the English Channel without a paddle.
MARIL.: Did the country fall on its knees to Khrushchev? Not by a long shot.
MARTHA: That's the very reason you two came to such bad ends, your minds are always in the gutter.
MARIL.: We're dead. We have the right to remain sentimental.
DOT.: The dead are not just sentimental, the dead understand the significance of sentimentality.
MARTHA: The dead can afford to be sentimental: they don't have to write the thank-you notes.
MARIL.: *(Pause)* Well, aren't we Miss Smarty Pants with the one-liners this evening?
(DOT. *has taken out a hand mirror and is working on her make-up/hair.* MARIL. *does the same after a moment.)*
MARTHA: What are you two doing now? Primping Mr. President? Give me that mirror. My reflection is probably as thin as Count Dracula's. *(She looks into mirror.)* Lord, look at my hair!
DOT.: We can fix that in no time. *(She gets up and begins working on* MARTHA's *hair.)* When I was on the chitlin' circuit as a green teenager, I learned to fix hair. I learned everything too. Hot work and wet.
MARTHA: What is she talking about? Hot and wet?
MARIL.: Think about it. Straight hair gets wet work to get curly and curly hair gets . . .
MARTHA: I get it! I get it! I'm not too hep on that ghetto slang, honey.

DOT.: I can dig it, shugga bugga! (*She brushes* MARTHA's *hair.*)

MARTHA: (*Moans*) Uhmmmmmmmmm! I love it when you talk "black."

MARIL.: Is that soothing?

MARTHA: Whaaaa . . .?

DOT.: She said, does this soothe you?

MARTHA: Soothing . . . uhmmm, yes . . .

DOT.: I don't think she feels like talking right now.

MARIL.: I once went a whole day without speaking a word, but I allowed myself to moan whenever necessary.

DOT.: Monks in China go years without speaking. Centuries.

MARIL.: Golly, I couldn't do it. I'll be talking from my grave—talk, talk, talk.

DOT.: (*Concludes hair brushing.*) There. Give me that mirror! Marilyn, let her see the back. You can glimpse infinity looking mirror into mirror that way.

MARIL.: You look nice.

MARTHA: I don't want to see infinity. I've seen it already. I don't like it. It doesn't have a happy ending.

DOT.: My, don't we look pretty now.

MARTHA: Thank you, yes. Faded beauty is such a poignant thing. Fade in; fade out.

MARIL.: Tell me about it. Men were making bids to take my corpse out on the town to show it off in dramatically lit cocktail lounges wearing crystal white fur paid for by money made in shady enterprises.

MARTHA: That would be a sight I can live without seeing.

MARIL.: Lights are going out all over Los Angeles. Half of Hollywood is dead or dying and the other half is going fast. Like the old poem says, "not with a bang but a whisper."

DOT.: That's "whimper," and you should shut up about that . . .

MARTHA: She's right, you know; about something. Something . . .

DOT.: About what?

MARTHA: I hear you. (*Flashes*) The living will envy the dead . . .

MARIL.: Envy their lack of incandescence . . .

MARTHA: Yuck! It's horrible! Mass murder on a massive scale disguised as natural disaster. Gentrified genocide! Gentrified genocide!!! Ow! God, I think I'm having a reaction . . . (*She coughs violently.*)

DOT.: Better ring the nurse . . . (*She rings.*)

MARIL.: It's gonna be O.K. sugar, the nurse is coming.

MARTHA: OW! My eyelashes hurt!!! *(She covers her eyes.)*
(Puppet NURSE enters.)
MARIL.: Nurse! I think her medication is wearing thin.
DOT.: Better increase the dosage.
(NURSE adjusts tubes on MARTHA.)
MARIL.: All the intensive care in the world doesn't amount to a hill
of beans when it's all said and done . . . *(She sobs.)*
DOT.: Try to cheer up, Lorelei; there's a millionaire under every
tombstone.
(NURSE concludes business and exits.)
MARTHA: Thank you. Thank you; that's better. My heart has stopped
beating like a freight train, at least.
MARIL.: The care is so good in this hospital.
DOT.: I know what you mean, I think.
MARTHA: Well, I don't. I want to go home to my Royal Doulton! I
want to go home to my Blue Willow! Don't you understand?
DOT.: Sure we understand, honey, but we don't care. We're dead.
MARIL.: We could pretend to care, if that's what you want.
MARTHA: No, no, no, no! My lord; give me rest. You don't know what
it means to be without a man. That's the most cruel punishment
of all. John wasn't THAT bad. There's worse, believe me. And so
handsome too.
DOT.: I'd sure rather be without a man than without a clue.
MARTHA: I really need to write this down. I'll never remember it
later, I know.
MARIL.: I kept a journal once, in a nice little red plastic notebook. I
tried to write my everyday thoughts for the day in it, but whenever
I tried to write in it, the shadow of my hand fell across the page, it
drove me crazy; so I could never see what I was writing until after
my hand had moved away, and many times, when I moved my
hand away, the handwriting would be . . . not mine.
MARTHA: Then whose?
MARIL.: A man's. One of the founding fathers.
DOT.: I know it had to be somebody famous.
MARIL.: This shadow would fall across the page at all hours, day
or night, indoors or out. I tried writing with my left, but then I
couldn't read it at all.
MARTHA: Is this about anything, I hope?
DOT.: Wait a minute! You mean your subconscious was deliberately
short-circuiting your ability to make even accidental connections
with your dark self!?

MARTHA: I understand the connection between the Big Mac and the Brazilian rainforest!

DOT.: Who leaked it to her? Who! 'Fess up!!

MARTHA: For every Big Mac sold, an acre of rainforest bites the dust, taking with it three species of iridescent beetles!

MARIL.: Incandescent.

DOR.: Don't you get it? For every evolutionary dead end street, there's a freeway to paradise, just over the horizon . . .

MARIL.: There are certain people who think that paradise isn't good enough for certain people . . .

DOR.: That must be what my horoscope meant this morning when it said, "avoid certain people with short memories."

MARTHA: I hope you weren't referring to me with that crack. I have a memory like an elephant with a broken heart.

MARIL.: You forgot about the truth . . .

MARTHA: What truth?

DOR.: Too much of it can deprive you of more than earthly comfort.

MARTHA: All I said was the FBI and the underworld killed those awful Kennedy brothers, and that crazy Martin Luther King. If I know about it, others must know about it too; and eventually the whole world will know, and that will signal the end of American life as we know it. The American dream will turn into a cartoon nightmare: that's all folks!

MARIL.: Eartha Kitt told the truth to Lady Bird Johnson, and Eartha never worked again.

MARTHA: Can we please get on with this! I'm ready to go. I'm ready to go now. You gals, thanks for all your help, I mean it. You tried. You really did, but . . .

DOR.: Yeah, right. We can take a hint. Let's go Miss Monroe.

MARIL.: Was it me? Was it something I said?

DOT.: (*To MARIL.*) Come on. We've got to finish our rounds, kitten. (*To MARTHA*) You're not the only fish in the frying pan, you know.

MARTHA: Go, go! Get out! That samba music is starting again! I feel dizzy! Let's get on with this! Let's get down to the real nitty-gritty, for God's sake.

DOR.: Come on Marilyn, I need some air and a smoke. It smells bad in here. (*She coughs as they go.*)

MARTHA: (*Rings call bell*) Where is she?! My medication is wearing off, I can feel myself getting real cranky. (*Rings again*) I want to go before I . . . (CARMEN *enters*) It's about time. I thought they'd never leave.

CARMEN: Que pasa, Chica? Did those girls lift your spirits in any significant way?

MARTHA: I'm afraid not. I'm afraid I'm beyond consolation and beyond a cure. I've said to John over and over: this government is not afraid to make people sick. Selected people, sick as a dog unto death. And they will not hesitate to do so, at the drop of a hat. I'm dying proof of it, right here. Where were you?

CARM.: Something came up.

MARTHA: I'm ready to go. I've been ready for hours. And it's unspeakably rude of you to keep me waiting . . . I don't want to live in another world without manners.

CARM.: There's a problem. A, eh, traffic problem.

MARTHA: I don't want to hear about it! Just get me out of here before I lose what's left of my mind . . .

CARM.: Believe me, I would like nothing better than to take you to the next level of being, Chica, but there is a glut of spirits jamming the entrance. This happens from time to time. Do not be alarmed. You see, it's due to the excessive number of unscheduled deaths. Rather embarrassing. The guards at the gates of the underworld have all had Secret Service training, so I'm sure . . .

MARTHA: I don't want to hear about the underworld. I know all about it. The Secret Service kept me from living, but I'll be damned if they keep me from dying.

CARM.: Yeah, they're regular princes of irony, and they don't even know it. But look, I'm working on something—a deal for you.

MARTHA: What deal? The time for dealing is done. Who are you dealing with? The Devil himself? Just what are we talking about, and don't give me any more false promises.

CARM.: Give me your hand, and close your eyes. I want to show you something . . .

MARTHA: Don't squeeze; I'm a sick woman. Now what?

CARM.: Here it comes; reception is pretty bad, but in a second you should . . .

MARTHA: Lord have mercy . . .! Ow! They're burning my eyes. I can't stand to look anymore. (*She opens her eyes.*) Who are they? Plague victims? Casualties of Viet Nam?

CARM.: Not exactly. They are like you. This door is reserved for loyal citizens killed by their own rulers. But we'll have to be patient a little longer . . . I know! I will attack them with my Tutti Frutti charm.

MARTHA: I don't think you're all that charming.

CARMEN: That's not what I mean. Listen. Tutti Frutti is deep voodoo. Just ask Little Richard. (*She begins making a vive circle with a triangle in the center, using salt and colored powders.*) An overdressed dishwasher from Macon, Georgia, got into Tutti Frutti and forever changed the history of music while becoming simultaneously the King and Queen of Rock and Roll. Or ask Josephine Baker when you meet her in the next world. Ask her about that banana tutu. People think it was about penises. (*MARTHA gets back in bed.*) Most people think that as a rule, missing the point that it is the slow ripening of the fruit that protects the Brown Mother. Preserving her in fragrant fertility, girding her waist with the armor of its seeds, which in turn, surround the great seed living in the center of her heart. My Tutti Frutti crown, you see, is far more than an easy laugh at the expense of a despised culture. It is a big basket of survival insurance masquerading as stage business. It is the crowning triumph of nature over oppression, a banquet for the famished spirit! (*Sings as puppets do a strange dance.*)

I'd never lie to you,
Tutti Frutti is deep Voodoo
You know it's true
'Cause I never would lie to you

Tutti Frutti is a lighthouse light
When you're sailing through a stormy night
Tutti Frutti at the bottom of the Voodoo well.
If you don't understand,
That was Tutti Frutti's special plan,
If you're with it, then you're
Welcome to my Voodoo spell
Welcome to my Voodoo spell!

(*Dance and magic fire, smoke, and clouds. At end of ritual, music dissolves leaving only the drumbeat. Lights change to MARTHA on hospital bed. She tosses and turns violently, in a fevered state. She buzzes call button impatiently.*)

MARTHA: Where in the name of God IS somebody?? I am in entirely too much pain, and I have no intention of putting up with it any longer. (*Buzz*) Something is eating my bones! (*Buzz*) Something

very, very small and mean is munching my bones from the inside out; and it wasn't even invited for dinner! It wasn't even invited! Not for dinner! *(Buzz)* Not for dinner! Not for dinner! It wasn't invited for dinner!! *(Buzz)*
(Drums segue into a samba. CARMEN *joins dancers in a dance of death. Lights down)*

END OF ACT ONE

ACT TWO

(TV music. Lights dim on talk show set. MARTHA *sits reading over some papers during voice over.)*

V.O.: Afternoon, Mr. and Mrs. America and welcome to the Pat Collins Show! While Pat is on vacation, your host this week will be Richard M. Nixon's favorite phone pal, let's give her a warm Pat Collins Show Welcome . . .! MARTHA MITCHELL! *(Lights full on* MARTHA.*) (Canned applause)*

MARTHA: Helloooo! Thank ya'll and welcome to the show! And a special hello to my friends and family in Pine Bluff, Arkansas, watching us on KAGR-TV the Voice of Culture in the Agricultural South. They always said I ought to have my own show! And thank you Pat wherever you are, for taking some time off and letting me fill in for you for an entire week! Just between you and me and the gate post, Pat's ratings just ain't what they usedta' be, and since they were at their highest for the week that I co-hosted, who do they call when they need to get a few more million viewers to wave in the sponsors' faces? Three guesses and the first two don't count! What a week we have planned for you, too. Tomorrow's guests will be two of the president's favorite Negroes. The great Pearl Bailey and the fantabulous Sammy Davis Jr.! *(Applause)* That's right; they're gonna sing and dance up a storm, like always, so don't miss it. I know I won't. Then, later on we'll have one of Hollywood is grandest legends, Miss Gloria Swanson. *(Applause)* She'll be telling us a thing or two about those nasty Kennedys; also Bob Woodward and Carl Bernstein. *(Applause)* Two of our greatest living patriots will discuss Deep Throat with Linda Lovelace! *(Applause)* Wait a minute! Everybody knows that I'm deep throat, don't they? I thought everybody knew . . . Before I bring out my first guest, I would like to make a very public apology to the passengers and crew on Braniff Airlines flight 356 between Washington and Los Angeles, who had the bad luck to be on the same plane with me yesterday. The report in the *Washington Post* described me as hysterical. I assure you I was NOT hysterical. I had, during the flight, been soothed with five double vodka martinis, and I was calm as a mouse. I just felt that it was my duty to tell them about the bomb planted on the plane in the baggage compartment. The Watergate boys were out to kill me, and they didn't care who else got in the way. All I was trying to do was clear my conscience of any guilt for the deaths of more than a hundred innocent people. I had been told weeks ago that they were going to try to hit me. But they hate it when I figure it out. My spies are everywhere. So I know what happened; don't think I don't. They defused the bomb by remote control, just to make me out a liar and a fool. Some comedian had a wheelchair waiting for me on arrival. I didn't mind that, but the straitjacket was uncalled for; another attempt to smear me! What? Yeah, O.K.! They want me to go faster so, without further ado, let me bring out my first guest today, you know and love her antics for many years on the silver screen, here she is looking fabulous after being dead for nearly fifteen years. The Brazilian flying fortress herself, CARMEN MIRANDA.

(APPLAUSE. CARMEN enters wearing a tailored suit with a subdued turban and platform shoes. She and MARTHA hug like sisters. She sits.)

CARMEN: Thank you for that wonderful welcome!

MARTHA: I can't believe you're actually dead. You look wonderful! *(Applause)* But Groucho Marx says you never wear any underpants. Is he on the level?

CARMEN: Groucho! What a puto! Never trust a man who writes his own material.

MARTHA: What's a puto? Some South American something? I don't speak español except for "andale!"

CARMEN: I come originally from Portugal. That's in Europe, you know.

MARTHA: I know all about it, it's the place where those jellyfish come from, isn't it? Portuguese Man-o-Wars? *(Canned laugh.)* How do they like your movies back home in Rio?

CARMEN: Not too much. They prefer Grace Kelly and Eva Marie Saint.

MARTHA: Isn't that always the way. A prophetess without honor in her own hometown. I hope you are going to treat us to a number. Wouldn't you like to see Carmen do her hoochie coochie number, folks? (*Applause.*)

CARMEN: That's "tutti frutti." But I didn't come to sing and dance. I came to warn you. Trust no one. Not doctors. Nurses. Daughters, sons. Watch what you eat and drink. Prepare your own meals whenever you can. It may be already too late for precautions.

MARTHA: If you're trying to scare me, forget it. Masters have tried. Masters of Menace. Come on, just one little verse of "Ayi Yai Yai"! Folks! Beg her, beg her! That's what she wants. (*Applause*)

CARMEN: Well I'm really not dressed for it, and I am a little rusty in the hip . . . but ONE verse . . . O.K.?! (*Big applause.*)

(*Sings*)

If you try to do your duty
They'll take your heart away
So get yourself a lawyer
Make your will, without delay!

I Ayi ayi ayi ai ai ai ai F B Ayi
Si sisisisisisisi CIA
Put your affairs in order, right away!

(*APPLAUSE. CARMEN bows and exits. MARTHA stays on couch in dim light.*)

MARTHA: The nerve of her trying to scare me in full view of the American public. I don't panic that easy. With every insult, every shock, my resolve increases.

(*Sings*)

One day Death, I know, will come for me
Hat in hand, wearing a sheepish grin
Like a sweetheart new returned to me,
And I will say, "Do please, come in."
After fleeting conversation;
Fame and fashion, back-home news,
He'll give me an invitation
To a dance I can't refuse . . .

Danse Macabre!
Expect only the best
When you're dancing with death
In a Danse Macabre!

Danse Macabre!
Danse Bizarre
Like a Hollywood Star
With her heart in a jar
In a danse Bizarre.
Danse Bizarre!

Danse tabu!
I feel such success
When I'm dancing with death
When I dance with you!
Danse Tabu!

(MARTHA dances. Lights change to bed. She exits. MARILYN and DOROTHY are lying in the hospital bed center.)

MARIL.: The more I think about it, the madder I get. Why didn't they help me instead of making me, so to speak, the enemy. After all the money I made for the business. Billions.

DOT.: Those old guys don't care. I should have played Cleopatra. I knew it. Everybody knew it. It could have saved my life long enough for me to become a factor in the blaxploitation era. Imagine me in *Cleopatra Jones at The Casino of Gold!*

MARIL.: My imagination isn't so good anymore, but I'm working on it. What if the Kennedys got together with Clint Murchison, the Underground Mob, J. Edgar, the Fair Play for Cuba gang, and they convinced my psychiatrist that I had to be discreetly killed . . .

DOT.: Don't forget your housekeeper. I never trusted that woman.

MARIL.: It's not true, what everybody thinks about me and Bobby, you know. He respects my memory to this day.

DOT.: He's dead, you know. They put that colored boy in jail for it, just because he happened to pull the trigger . . .

MARIL.: What time is it?

DOT.: Late. How much does she know?

MARIL.: Not a lot. You know how Carmen is. Easy does it.

(CARMEN enters. Her costume combines elements of DR. and MIRANDA.)

CARM.: And now, ladies and women, here she is just like you remember her, drum roll please, the one, the only, Martha Bell Mitchell!

(MARTHA enters wearing her "Queen'" costume, complete with hat and parasol. She strikes a pose. Others stare in silence.)

MARTHA: What's the matter? Don't ya'll like it?

DOR.: Well, it's not exactly right for a funeral, is it?

CARM.: I told her . . .

MARTHA: This is my queen's dress. I wore it to meet her majesty Elizabeth Regina at Buckingham Castle and everything . . .

MARIL.: Did you shake hands with her? Her hands are so soft. Like a baby's.

DOR.: Yours would be too, if you never did a lick of work in your entire life.

MARIL.: Queens shouldn't have to work. It isn't royal.

DOR.: Honey, where did you get those open-toed sling-back pumps? They went out of style when I was alive.

MARTHA: I know. I had to have them specially made. Most comfortable shoe I've ever worn. I have several pairs made at the same time, all in white, then I dye 'em to match my outfits.

MARIL.: How clever of you.

MARTHA: Do you think the parasol's too much?

ALL: Oh no . . .

MARTHA: Good. I really want to make a first impression they'll never forget.

CARM.: I think you got it covered, Chica.

MARTHA: I never dreamed I'd have to talk my way into the inner circle of hell.

CARM.: It's not hell, it's . . .

MARTHA: Whatever you call it. It sure as hell's not the pearly gates of Eden.

DOR.: *(To CARM.)* What's she mean? You made a deal with them at the gate?

CARM.: Even with the bottleneck clogging the entrance to your destination, a way can always be found to slip one more spirit into the elevator.

MARIL.: They want to pick my brains . . .

CARM.: There is certain information; certain privileged information if you please, which Martha possesses, which the dwellers of the underworld would like in order to gain some lost ground in their endless underground wars . . .

MARTHA: Information that was leaked to me by a high-ranking Washington source, I might add.

DOR.: Good! Eternity has no ethics. Tell them everything you know, girl.

MARTHA: I'll tell some deep secrets, all right. See how they like them apples.

DOR.: Goodness, yes! You don't want to end up like us, do you? Guiding others to a land we can never know. It's worse than Greek tragedy.

MARIL.: I don't mind. I don't want to rest in peace forever.

CARM.: Don't worry, you won't.

MARTHA: I want to spill the beans all over the table. I want to tell ALL. I have a pipeline into the underworld conspiracy to overthrow the ancient gods. I mean really ancient.

CARM.: Why must they fight these wars of attrition, like cosmic Kamikazes in a lousy Warner Brothers propaganda movie.

DOR.: It's a side effect of having strong beliefs.

MARTHA: Sometimes I have the distinct impression that I'm dreaming this entire adventure, and in a moment, I'll wake up in my own bed on 5th Avenue, a little groggy from the alcohol and pills, but otherwise unscathed . . .

DOR.: I think that falls in the category of a fond wish.

CARM.: Say your au revoirs, and come along . . .

MARTHA: I'm ready . . .

MARIL.: Spill your guts out. You'll feel better right away. (CARM. *and* MARTHA *exit. A pause.*) Do you think of yourself as symbolic?

DOR.: Symbolic of what?

MARIL.: . . . Of anything . . . the durability of the Goddess, for instance.

DOR.: I don't believe that stuff anymore, after what I've seen. Forget it.

MARIL.: Men have no trouble thinking of themselves as symbols, then they forget what the symbols stand for.

DOR.: Not only men do that, honey. My mother was addicted to symbols of prestige and middle-class comfort. She drank secretly until she died of it, quite in the open. But not before she saw me develop into the perfect object of desire.

MARIL.: I don't want to stand for anything anymore. Not for sexy youth, not tragedy, not mysterious death. Not for anything anymore, but me: standing alone!

DOR.: Yeah, but who do you think would pay to see that?

(CARMEN *enters.*)

CARMEN: . . . And now, here she is, just like you're . . .

MARIL.: What happened? Did she get in? (MARTHA *enters.*) I guess not.

DOT.: What happened, honey?

MARTHA: It wasn't real pleasant . . .

116

CARMEN: J. Edgar Hoover, JFK, Jimmy Hoffa, LBJ, RFK, and MLK plus three stooges from the CIA, the Mafia, and the Tri-Lateral Commission sitting around a big table looking very smug . . .

MARTHA: I sat down and began to speak my piece. There's a conspiracy, I said, a dreadful conspiracy among the lords of darkness to keep the righteous from rising to cabinet-level positions! To pack the Supreme Court with lower echelon demons intent on the spread of godless communism in the celestial regions. Contaminating heaven with filth! I tried to control my emotions, but it was sure hard. I told them, if only I were given free passage across the border checkpoint, I would personally see to it that such dangerous tendencies come to an end. Such an imbalance would undermine the very fabric of time and space; I pleaded with them. It's one thing to give the devil his due, but lately he's been taking more! Much more!

DOT.: How did they take that?

MARTHA: It was infuriating! Hoffa did all the talking. He never liked me.

MARIL.: Well . . .?

MARTHA: He just looked embarrassed for a minute, smiled at me with those yellow teeth and said, "Gossip is without currency. Look within."

DOT.: And . . .?

CARMEN: That was it.

MARIL.: Look within?

MARTHA: Do you believe it? Look fucking within. How patronizing. But instead of getting angry, I just fell asleep right at the table from the deadening effect of accumulated weariness. Went out like a lighthouse. Next thing I know, I'm standing here talking to you. Now I'll never get home. (*She weeps.*)

DOT.: Don't give up, there might be another way! (*To* CARM.) Do you tell her, or shall I?

MARIL.: Oh, you poor woman. I can't watch! (*Turns her back.*)

CARM.: There is . . . eh, one more chance maybe . . .

DOT.: Spit it out!

CARM.: (*She spits.*) Come with me. (*She takes* MARTHA's *hand and leads her to* MARIL., *who turns around and begins to shudder,* CARMEN *places a pipe in* MARIL.'s *mouth. Image of John Mitchell on video.*)

MARTHA: John . . .? Oh JOHN! I knew you'd come for me! How'd you get here, anyway?

CARM.: I can't watch this . . . (*She walks off.*)

MARTHA: Wait a minute; did you let 'em suck you in? Oh John, honey, are you one of them? Oh God! Oh my GOD! I have terminal cancer and my hero is the devil himself.

MARIL. as JOHN: No devil. Just a man on a mission.

MARTHA: How could you say all that stuff about me? Mean, awful things you said to the press! To the press!!

JOHN: You've let yourself go a little.

MARTHA: Well, are you dead too, or what?

JOHN: That comes later. Some of us know how to go, you know, back-and-forth.

MARTHA: My word! Nobody told me . . . What have you become? A yes-man for the forces of negativity!

JOHN: Just listen for a minute. Listen. The fellows brought me out here to tell you; they asked me to tell you, really, well, you're not going. Not going in.

MARTHA: In? What?

JOHN: The door! The blasted door, Martha!! For Christ's sake, don't you see? They're really pissed off at you. Really extremely PISSED! You know? So the deal came down: let her rot.

MARTHA: That can't be. Not after what I've been through, there must be some mistake. (*Suddenly angry*) I gave you everything I had! Everything! My soul! And YOU! You nailed it to the wall and used it for target practice!

JOHN: I'm so ashamed. Not about that mess; I should have, controlled, you know, controlled you better. Should have done a better job in front of the fellas. If I had, Mr. President would still be Mr. President, and we wouldn't be having this little discussion.

MARTHA: Didn't you love me enough to save me from myself? Were you blinded by presidential loyalty?

JOHN: It was too much, just, just too too much! The President! Everything! I did what I could do. Not much. Mr. President hated women. Hated you. Hated your childish power. He lost respect for me because of you. Just lost it. I began to hate you, too, because of it.

MARTHA: You turned my little girl against me, didn't you? My little baby.

JOHN: She was turning into a scale model of you! One monster in the family was plenty! I rescued her, for what it's worth, and she THANKS me for it!

MARTHA: I didn't try to screw it up, Daddy; I really didn't TRY to . . .!

JOHN: With a good deal of personal satisfaction, I inform you that your long awaited romp through Elysian Fields has been put on indefinite hold.

MARTHA: But I don't want to ROMP; I want a good night's sleep. You don't understand anything! You just don't! (*She collapses in his lap. Lights change, wing chair goes away. MARTHA is alone on the floor. MARIL. and DOT. enter and cross to MARTHA..*)

MARIL.: Don't cry, pussycat, no politician is worth it!

MARTHA: Thank God! I thought I was alone, for good.

DOT.: You'll never be alone again, darling.

MARTHA: I don't want to go to limbo. My back won't bend that far. My back won't take it, you don't understand.

DOT.: We'll do everything for you. Whatever you need just name it, just . . . (*DOT. and MARIL. assist MARTHA to her feet, they straighten her clothes and wipe her tears away.*)

MARIL.: Feel free to call on us, anytime. We'll do everything we can, which is a lot.

(*CARMEN enters dressed as the Angel of Death. She opens her arms to MARTHA. MARIL. and DOT. exit. Music.*)

MARTHA: My REAL life, I've kept totally inside me. I've never spoken a word about it to anybody. That's the life I see flashing before me now, from day one. Signposts, landmarks of an inner nature, uncontaminated by articulation. The life of the spirit is . . . very mysterious.

CARM.: Now the living woman disappears, to let the legend breathe.

(*MARTHA enters her embrace, and holds tightly. Lights out*)

Epilogue

(*Changes back to hospital room as at scene one. NURSE 1 and NURSE 2 are prepping for a new patient.*)

MARIL./NURSE 2: I'm usually right, but sometimes they fool me, even the terminal ones.

DOT./NURSE 1: Yeah, you get a sense of who's going to make it and who's not, after you see 'em come in and out for a while. I thought she would fight her way back. She was sure mean enough to.

NURSE 2: I know. What a mouth, huh? I feel funny.

NURSE 1: Funny?

NURSE 2: Yeah. Like she's just down the hall. Like she never died at all, you know.

NURSE 1: There are worse things than dying. If you don't know what they are, you haven't really lived.

(DR. MONTALVO *enters and pulls back bed curtain;* MARTHA *is gone. She goes to foot of bed and reads chart.*)

DR. MONTALVO: That will be all.

(NURSES *exit. Samba music starts softly and builds as* DR. M. *gets into the bed and pulls sheets over her head, as lights fade to out.*)

THE END